SEAN BYRNE

Esoteric Christianity

A Tragic History

The Church's holy war against
the spirit of Sophia

By the same author:

Poems for the Path (verse)
Patrick and the Holy Grail (fiction)
Gnosis! (fiction)

SEAN BYRNE

Esoteric Christianity
A Tragic History

The Church's holy war against
the spirit of Sophia

AGE-OLD
BOOKS

THIS BOOK IS DEDICATED TO
ALL TRUE SEEKERS OF THE SPIRIT IN OUR TIME

Published by AGE-OLD BOOKS in Northern Ireland

Contact: **ageoldbooksinfo@gmail.com**

Author's Email: **byrnesean594@gmail.com**

ISBN: 978-0-9540255-5-7

A catalogue record of this book is available from the British Library.

Cover design by Ray Lipscombe

www.seanbyrne.net

CONTENTS

PART ONE

THE FIRST MILLENNIUM: A STRUGGLE FOR UNITY

PART TWO

THE SECOND MILLENNIUM: A LEGACY OF CONFLICT

A GOOD MAN,

THROUGH OBSCUREST ASPIRATION,

HAS STILL AN INSTINCT OF THE ONE TRUE WAY.

Goethe's FAUST

INTRODUCTION

Christianity takes many forms. This book attempts to elucidate and outline the historical development of a lesser known but surely one of the most mysterious and fascinating forms of this great spiritual/religious movement: Esoteric Christianity.

Esoteric Christianity differs from mainstream Christianity in a number of significant ways. One is that it reveals fundamental and relevant information and knowledge pertaining to the essence of Christianity which has never gained a wide currency. From about the middle of the 4th century onwards, precise knowledge of the spirit or the hidden spirit-world, a knowledge upon which Christianity was actually founded, was discouraged and later actively suppressed. Eventually, it almost totally disappeared from public view.

Another important aspect of Esoteric Christianity is that it places Christianity itself into a much deeper and wider historical context than is usual. In doing this it also reveals

Christianity as a religion which, though centred upon the historical event of the Incarnation, actually is rooted in a spiritual tradition much more ancient than this.

Esoteric Christianity can thus be said to be 'perennialist' in nature. This means among other things that it represents that aspect of Christianity which can transcend what conventionally separates it from other religions, because it is a form of Christianity which gives a Christian expression to something which is in fact a universal experience: the thirst for true knowledge of the divine spirit, knowledge of man's true origins, make-up, and destiny, something which has always, from time immemorial, expressed itself as a desire to know that Being that we, for simplicity's sake, always refer to as God.

It can thus be truly said of Esoteric Christianity that it represents a path which makes the realisation of this aspiration possible for all people, no matter who, what or where they are, for it points the way to that secret yet accessible wisdom of God the soul of man invariably longs for. And though it does this by placing the figure of Christ at its centre, Esoteric Christianity nevertheless can be said to represent the deepest yet common core of all true religion. This somewhat paradoxical statement will become clear in the course of the book. Indeed, in this perhaps lies Esoteric Christianity's greatest virtue! For living as we do in a time when a superficial or even fanatical fundamentalism in faith and beliefs is on the increase in many places, the spirit of Esoteric Christianity offers a way of circumventing or transcending these unwelcome trends. It offers the possibility of avoiding the dogmatic intransigence established religions often display in high, or even low places, while yet having the advantage of remaining true to the spiritual core of all of these religions. Furthermore, Esoteric Christianity establishes a spiritual way or path which the doubtful and even those of no religious persuasion may well be able to relate to. For while retaining what is most essential to the practise of religion and spirituality generally, it yet of necessity does not demand of its adherents any obligatory or cultic practises. These often indeed do as much to divide people from one another than to unite them. Esoteric Christianity gives expression to *perennial* truths which constitute the very essence of every human being's true make-up. Furthermore, these are truths which must of necessity go to the inmost heart of all spiritual matters. In doing this, Esoteric Christianity provides the soundest basis possible upon which religious, ethnic and especially purely human barriers, of whatever kind, can come down and become entirely a thing of the past. It is thus a path of great promise.

All this is possible because at the centre of Esoteric Christianity lies the knowledge of an art, a science even, which contains the very essence of what is most needed in the world: the art or science of true healing.

This healing is possible because Esoteric Christianity offers the tools and techniques of an essentially spiritual or divine art which is nothing less than the spirit of pure enlightenment and knowledge. It is, or was, a spirit which once lived very vibrantly in Christianity, especially during the time of Christ's physical presence on the Earth and for a couple of centuries afterwards. What we now rather diffusely call 'the Church' was itself, one can justly say, born and grew up out of this spirit and also provided the foundation of all that came afterwards. This early foundational period is now generally known as The Gnosis.[1]

After this time, however, this spirit rapidly diminished and for complex reasons was eventually almost snuffed out. This was a tragedy of the first degree!

Tracing the reasons for this tragedy, as this book attempts to do, is thus also an attempt to describe the history and demise of the human/divine spirit itself! The issues are indeed very complex, but the book attempts nevertheless to simplify them, so that in understanding their essentials the true spirit of Christianity, which is also the Holy Spirit of Sophia, can manifest once again and thereby lead souls forward in a vital mission at this time: the work of the healing of the Earth and its peoples.

PART ONE

THE FIRST MILLENNIUM:
A STRUGGLE FOR UNITY

CHAPTER ONE

THE IMPORTANCE OF SOPHIA
TO THE FIRST CHRISTIANS

———ooooOoooo———-

In attempting to understand both the original essence of Christianity and the salient features of its spiritual, as opposed to its purely temporal, history, it is necessary to call attention to two general aspects of it. One is that from its very beginning Christianity had two distinct 'flavours' which can be characterized as Eastern and Western. Another key point to be kept in mind is the importance ascribed in early Christianity to the *feminine* aspect or concept of God, or the Divine Feminine. In the East, this was summed up in the Being known as 'Sophia'. In the West, where early Christianity came to its greatest flowering in the Irish Celtic Church of the 5th to the 8th centuries, the same Being was recognized as an aspect of the ancient Goddess Brigid.

These points are important because they have a direct relationship to the balance, purity, brilliance, and strength of the spirit of the early Church. But also, and equally importantly, they relate directly to why this spirit was subsequently largely quenched.

The overall religious tradition out of which Christianity was conceived and into which it was born and had subsequently to find its feet, i.e. the ancient Mosaic/Judaic tradition, had little place in it for the feminine. This, however, was not the case with the so-called gentile religions which surrounded the Jews and of which they were suspicious and even fearful. For in these the feminine, or one can say, the soul or fecund aspect, held much greater sway than the more intellectual, spiritual, or 'logos'[2] element that the Jews cultivated. Similarly, if we look at the situation in the West, we find also that the feminine played a very important part in the religions of the time, as even a cursory knowledge of the myths and legends, often the basis of these various cults, will show.

Thus, when Christianity eventually came to Ireland, it found waiting, so to speak, a maternal embrace, something which it was in effect largely denied within the strict tradition out of which it was born. Furthermore, this feminine atmosphere remained very strong in Hibernia compared with other places in the then known world. The reasons for this are several, but nevertheless had very much to do with the fact that the Hibernians never came under the direct, restrictive influence of the patristic Roman world with all its attendant trappings of male aggressiveness and militaristic imperialism. Yet of all these, in truth spiritually repressive influences played very strongly into the early

Christian drama in Palestine where the presence of Rome was ubiquitous.

Thus we can see that the formative cultural and spiritual forces of the time and place of the enactment of the Incarnation were both monotheistic (Jewish) and male orientated (Jewish or Roman). However, partly because of the light in which Christ came to be seen in early Christianity, with regard to the feminine as a divine aspect of the Godhead, the Church soon began to take on a wholly different character to Patriarchal Judaism.

THE GNOSIS

The reason why this feminine element entered into Christianity at all is that from the very beginning, Christ was seen to represent something new, exciting, and totally different in religion generally, something which seemed to both transcend and at the same time unite elements that were previously divisive in the spiritual life of man. This perception was very much to do with the familial or community aspect of early Christian life. However, it was a 'family' that was not, as it was previously and in all peoples, based on blood-ties, but a purely spiritual bonding which transcended those ties. The early Christian community was very diverse in this sense.

The New Testament is at pains in many places to point out there can be no Christian life at all without this new concept of community life, and in the early Church this spiritual ideal was truly lived. This impulse for family and community is, it need hardly be said, far more feminine than masculine.

It has to be remembered, too, that early Christianity in Palestine manifested itself as one of the main tenets within a confluence of diverse religions and philosophical systems which flourished in the general area of the Middle East between approximately the 1st century B.C. and the 3rd century A.D. and which has come to be known as The Gnosis.

Initially, however, Christianity was seen to form part of the Judaic culture. But what is most important to understand in relation to how Christianity began to assert its fundamental difference from the Gentile-fearing Jews, is that at the centre-point of the thriving Gnosis was a spiritual Being who represented none other than the feminine aspect of the supreme Godhead itself. The name which was given to this Being was Sophia. Early Christianity thrived on Sophia because she had the power, so natural to her gender, not only to break old moulds, but to do so in an entirely wise and enlightened fashion.

Furthermore, Sophia occupied a primary place in the consciousness, hearts and souls of the first highly inspired followers of Christ because she combines into one those twin aspects of divinity most essential to the pursuit of any spiritual path of knowledge that leads to God: Wisdom and Love, which together represent 'philosophia', or philosophy. In Greek, 'phileo' means love and 'sophia' means wisdom. To the Greeks, it must be pointed out, philosophy was not the abstract pursuit which we have come to know it as. To them 'philosophia' was a living or divine spiritual Being, a Goddess in fact. Both Phileo (Love) and Sophia (Wisdom) are essentially and fairly easily identifiable as being purely feminine.

All of this figured very strongly in the spiritual dynamics of the formation of the early Church. As it developed, however, much of the old patriarchal Judaism and its law-orientated and custom-ridden influence inevitably lingered on. Though now transformed and in possession of a new Christian countenance, patriarchism nevertheless, as time passed, tended to increasingly oppress the wonderful new, fresh, pure, and feminine power. This patriarchism was something which ran very deep indeed and could hardly but at some point have become the cause of tension and conflict within the emergent forms of early Christianity. Thus we may easily imagine the kinds of social and personal difficulties which erupted as the ancient male-orientated traditions, customs, and attitudes became challenged within the new Sophia-infused milieu. Furthermore, we can very easily imagine tempers and emotions running high as the aggressive male element once more tried to gain the upper hand after the initial flood of Sophia-inspired freedom had subsided, and indeed this is what happened! There is much in the letters of the New Testament to indicate that these kinds of problems existed even from the very beginning.

The Sophia power was novel, strong and widespread. It promised much possibility for change, perhaps far too much for some, and was thus perceived as something of a threat also. As it turned out, these forces of reaction gathered themselves slowly but surely within the growing Church and at length they gained the upper hand. Soon a rehashed partiarchism was emerging as the new Church's strongest power. Moreover, it was a power exceedingly conscious of its own far-reaching possibilities and was hell-bent on consolidating itself.

A FOUL CRIME

Everyone knows just how deeply the antagonisms between the sexes can run! But when feelings like these are hitched onto spiritual and political causes, they can give rise to crises that reach far beyond the personal and can even affect the course of history itself.

The depths of jealousy and spiritual hatred which this masculine Judaic/Roman consciousness could inspire against the spirit of Sophia is well illustrated and symbolized by one of the Church's earliest and foulest crimes. This concerned the sagacious and beautiful philosopher Hypatia.

Let us briefly consider her case therefore, for it indicates well just what was happening in the Church at this time.

By the 5th century the Sophia-loving Gnostics were well and truly rooted out, and in the emerging Church the new style of a purely Christian patriarchism, which the Gnostics' defeat was rapidly breeding, began in earnest to tackle feminism. Attitudes were becoming increasingly hardened, intolerant, and even fanatical.

Hypatia was one of the most renowned and influential teachers in the famous neo-platonic School of Alexandria where the last vestiges of the Gnostic wisdom still lingered, and had the power to provoke bitter dispute between factions engaged in what was fast becoming a battle for the very survival of the true sophianic spirit of the early Church. Because Hypatia could evoke, through her wisdom, eloquence and vast learning, a powerful image of the sublime Sophia herself, she fell foul of the anti-feminists of whom the zealous Church Father (St.) Cyril was undoubtedly the most vicious. It was he, history tells us, who orchestrated and incited a crazed mob to perform a deed more ugly than one can imagine and destroy this lovely vessel of inspired wisdom and purity!

Cyril was Bishop of Alexandria at the time in question. The author of many books on theology and against heresy, he was one of the chief architects of the eventually triumphant Roman orthodoxy. Obviously incensed that one of her gender could achieve such fame, authority, and spiritual influence as Hypatia undoubtedly had in the city where he himself was busily consolidating and strengthening the growing and highly patriarchal Roman-inspired Church, Cyril resorted to the foulest of all tactics to rid himself of her. Into the minds of a carefully manipulated band of the fanatical rabble – so-called monks – who lived in various communities in the outlying districts of the great city, he implanted seeds of spiritual hatred against Hypatia, and these he carefully nurtured until the time was ripe for his vile plan to take effect. Then, at the appropriate moment, and on foot of a signal from Cyril, this mob was incited to such a pitch that they attacked Hypatia, 'dragged her off the street and into a church and there stripped her naked and hacked her to death with oyster shells, after which she was torn to pieces and her limbs carried to a place called Cineron and there burned to ashes' (415 A.D.).

Such was the tragic fate of one of the brightest jewels of Neo-Platonism.

Though by the time of Hypatia's prominence, Alexandria and its famous School were long in decline, due largely to the Roman occupation and influence of which Cyril was a prime representative, the School and the city were nevertheless still a matrix of the deepest religious, philosophical, and spiritual fervour. However, it was also a milieu in which the proud and growing young Christian Church felt itself constantly threatened by what it increasingly regarded as heretical beliefs and practices. It thus felt the need to define and defend its own particular beliefs ever more clearly against those whom it deemed, rightly or wrongly, to be its opponents. The manner in which it set about doing this is undoubtedly connected with the male-dominated culture in which it was trying to grow. While it is not here suggested that Cyril's was the *principal* method of achieving it, nevertheless the Church's orthodoxy gained momentum far more through the masculine power of 'theologia' than through the sublime and richer influence of 'philosophia' and her inspired Neo-Platonists. Unable, therefore, to properly incorporate this feminine soul/spiritual wisdom into its doctrines and dogmas, the Church as a result became ever more temporally inclined and power-orientated, more male-dominated and heretic-fearing. In this atmosphere, the gentle and maternal spirit of Sophia gradually lost her power and influence and sadly eventually faded almost completely from sight, to be cultivated only by those espousing that form of Christianity which we here call esoteric.

THE ANCIENT MYSTERY RELIGIONS AND THEIR RELEVANCE TO CHRISTIANITY

One of the main, if not *the* main reason why Sophia, as representative of the Divine Feminine, played such an important role in The Gnosis was her connection with the very ancient mystery religions of mankind. Because Christianity arose directly out of Judaism, a religion whose deepest wisdom can in turn be traced directly back to these ancient mystery religions, it is necessary to have some knowledge of them if we wish to understand just where the original spirit of Christianity came from and what it stood for. Therefore, before we try to expose more fully this spirit of early Christianity, let us pause briefly to look at this particular 'mystery' phenomenon of the ancient world.

It is true to say that nearly every ancient culture and nation had its own Mysteries or mystery religion. Whether a nation or a tribal grouping was primitive in the extreme or whether it reached the sophisticated heights attained by, for example, the ancient Egyptians, religion was always the form in which man's most basic cultural and civilizing tendencies were experienced, expressed, and fostered. Needless to say, these Mysteries differed widely in style and content and actually acquired their particular characteristics according to the folk who adhered to them or the geographic location in which they manifested. There was, however, at least one fundamental principle which underpinned and was common to all of them. And this, significantly, is a principle which still holds good even today, for it has a psychological validity appertaining directly to man's religious impulse, though in our own time it of necessity takes on a very different character. What we refer to is the principle of *initiation*.

It will thus be seen when investigating these old Mysteries that they invariably had an outer as well as an inner form. The outer forms were chiefly those rites, ceremonies and practices performed publicly and usually in accordance with the rhythms of the changing seasons. The inner forms, however, were always enacted in strictest secrecy. The overall form was perpetuated by the leaders of the Mysteries who periodically separated out from the masses some few individuals of exceptional promise, expressly to initiate them into the secret meanings of the various ceremonial or cultic practices which, though known to all, were rarely understood. These festivities and sacred observances were always arranged and orchestrated by the leaders of the Mysteries. The ordering of the community, through the exercise of religious, mystical or even magical power over the mass of people, was the prerogative of the Initiate, for he was the one with the great power of the inner knowledge at his disposal.

Thus it can be said that initiation always signified the existence of a hidden or secret civilizing knowledge. Even more importantly, it pointed to the manner in which this knowledge was acquired. This is also the reason why the ancient religions are known as the Mysteries.

Those who passed the necessary initiatory tests and thus acquired the mystery knowledge were known by different names in different cultures and religions, e.g. priests, priest-kings, hierophants, druids or shamans, etc. However, the generic name which can cover all of these is 'initiate.'

This is the way in which the initiates nearly always became a powerful grouping in ancient societies. In the most advanced of these societies, nations or tribes, there can be no question at all as to the initiates' primary and formative influence. Thus, if we trace the Semitic current of mankind back to ancient Egypt, we find flourishing there, even four thousand years before our own era, one of the world's most sophisticated of initiation-based cultures.

MONOTHEISM – THE KEY SPIRITUAL CONCEPT

Here we have, if you like, the method by which all civilization on the Earth gradually arose. Before civilization proper, man lived in a kind of dreamlike, half-earthy, half-cosmic condition, where he felt just as much at home with the gods as he did on the Earth itself. It may have been inwardly paradisal; outwardly, however, his life was instinctive, tribal and often brutish, and if he was ever going to evolve beyond this, things had to change!

Thus, out of the primeval and mysterious depths of time when man begins his fascinating and often tortuous journey on the face of the Earth, historians and anthropologists can, through studying the mythic content of the Mysteries, give us some little taste of the cosmic consciousness of the ancients and their grand initiation wisdom.

What a consciousness it was! For, as the old stories and myths invariably show, the soul of the ancients was imbued with a fabulous knowledge of gods and goddesses, of spiritual and elemental beings, a consciousness overflowing with wild and passionate life, and one which came to its greatest expression and clarity in the souls of the initiates and their disciples.

As the aeons passed and great cultures and civilizations rose and fell, they invariably made an impact upon the larger consciousness and culture of mankind. At the same time, they left, especially through their religions, traces of their wisdom and knowledge, traces that we, even to this day, may examine with profit.

Although the Eleusinian, Samothracian, Hibernian, and various other Mysteries all have played their part in the development of human culture and consciousness, it was the Semites who bequeathed to our modern culture its most singular, salient, and beneficent spiritual feature, for it is to these peoples, especially those who elaborated the great spiritually based culture and civilization of ancient Egypt, that we owe our knowledge of the primary spiritual concept of *monotheism*.

Monotheism is, one could say, the very first theological pillar upon which the Christian religion is or was raised. Of all the ancient religious traditions, it was this concept that was the most highly developed and elaborated in the temples of Egypt. It was upon the recognition that there was fundamentally only One, though often an unknown, God, behind the many others who invariably vied for their attention and allegiance, that the Egyptians built their civilization. Through this concept, and the unifying effect it had on their consciousness, the Egyptian Initiates achieved for their civilization its great sophistication. With this key in their possession, the Egyptian priest-initiates could unlock the ordered spiritual power necessary to control and channel the often chaotic pantheism and polytheism which was the most pronounced feature of the various tribes within their jurisdiction. In this way, the Initiates could promote their civilization and direct its evolution in whatever way they desired.

CHAPTER TWO

THE PERENNIAL WISDOM-PHILOSOPHY AND THE COMING OF CHRIST

———ooooOoooo———-

Although monotheism has come to us via the line of descent described briefly in the previous chapter, i.e. through the Semites and the Egyptians, then via Moses and the Jews into the beginnings of Christianity, it must be pointed out that at the heart of all the great Mysteries of antiquity this concept also lived. It may indeed be said that monotheism represents the very core of the ancient and perennial wisdom-philosophy[3] and that it is the foundation of an esoteric doctrine which is common to all great religions. It is true that it takes on different forms according to time and place, but although it is elaborated here in this book under the name of Christ, the merely outward name should never be an obstacle to realizing its sublime inner truth.

It is perhaps understandable that conventional Christianity will proudly and resolutely proclaim its God, Jesus Christ, as the *only* God, or the *only* Son of God, etc. Such a practise is, after all, indicative of the very nature of what we call monotheism. What is generally missing, however, from such a proclamation is an informed understanding of how it differs from other versions of monotheism. Let it be said from the outset that such an uninformed overemphasis is merely divisive as far as getting to the heart of the matter of the One universal God is concerned. Thus, as far as the brother-and-sisterhood implications of the concept of monotheism can be made to apply practically in the world, an empty or a fundamentalist insistence on a single *name* without the necessary wisdom-informed elaboration of its true meaning, will merely add to the existing confusion and divisions. The danger of this mis-emphasis on the part of conventional Christianity is something which only an understanding of Esoteric Christianity can make fully apparent.

The questions involved here are highly complex. It must be noted, however, that these were the very same kinds of questions which the early Christian Gnostics tried to tackle. But unlike in our time, they tried to do this in a meaningful and comprehensive way. We may thus designate these considerations as 'perennial', for they call into question the Godhood or divinity of Christ himself and in doing so highlight the need to properly address and define Christ's relationship to other messianic figures, prophets, avatars, etc.

The Gnostic Church, however, thrived on this kind of debate and did so because of its essential spirit of goodwill towards the Incarnation. It was only gradually that this spirit of goodwill began to give way to a much more hard-headed and dogmatic approach to the whole question, or set of questions. Moreover, it was this dogmatic tendency that represented those forces at work within Christianity which moved to outlaw Gnosticism.

From an esoteric point of view this was a fundamental error! Essentially what this outlawing of Gnosticism and the promotion of dogmatism did was to try to reduce the relevance of the Incarnation to a mere matter of words or definition of terms. This was in direct contravention of the essence of the Incarnation, which should not be reduced to merely human definitions or word-formulas.

St. Paul makes this very clear in his letter to the Galatians (see Galatians 1:10-12). The spiritual essence of the Incarnation lies in the fact that it actually *happened*; it is not, therefore, so much a teaching as a fact of spiritual life! That, he emphasizes, is the point!

THE MUMMIFICATION OF THE TRUTH

It can therefore be said that intellectualism, dogmatism, and so forth, often do nothing more than fudge the real issues. For it is undoubtedly the case that after the light of The Gnosis was quenched the Church tried to put the living truth about Christ into a mere set of formulas, articles of faith, and so on. It did this because instinctively it knew the truth had to be preserved in some way for future generations, but in doing this it also in a sense mummified the living truth into laws and lifeless word-formulas. These formulas have their part to play in the Christian religion, but the danger is that they appeal only or usually to the head, to intellectual types, to the exclusion of the 'common man', and often to the detriment of the deepest needs of all.

Esoteric Christianity has the potential and the means to address these deeper needs which, from a spiritual as well as a physical point of view, are in essence far more to do with real blood and real flesh than with mere words!

We shall look later at this blood aspect of the Incarnation much more closely, but for now suffice it is to say that with even a cursory knowledge of the often absurd debates that go on and have gone on in the past regarding the true nature of the Christ Being, that this in itself indicates the manner in which the spirit of the early Church inevitably and so sadly got lost to the common man or woman, and a kind of watered-down or idolized version of him, not very different from other gods, was put in place.

Briefly stated, in the early Church all of the trends indicated above eventually coalesced into the superstructures of the emerging orthodoxy, which represented the triumph of a male-orientated intellectualism over a female, and much more soul-orientated, spiritualism.[4]

THE DIVINE TRINITY

Before proceeding further into the history of the deep esoteric spirit, we must consider another important doctrinal issue which also figured strongly in early Christianity: the question of the Holy Trinity. We need to address this, however briefly, because it is a fundamental issue towards which we must gain a positive relationship if we are to fully comprehend the true nature of both Esoteric Christianity and its conventional shadow.

The Trinity may be represented as the second theological pillar upon which the temporal Church raised itself in the world. Thus, a study of the early Church will also reveal its preoccupation with this controversial doctrinal issue. It is important because it is an issue that is directly connected with monotheism, as well as being a fundamental plank of all the ancient Mystery wisdom-teachings. Unlike the later elaboration of the Christian Trinity, however, the ancient Mystery teaching of the Trinitarian nature of the Godhead was a doctrinal concept that incorporated both the masculine and feminine principles, and also their fusion, embodied in the principle of sonship in Christianity.

What is central to an understanding of the history of Esoteric Christianity is that this exclusion of the feminine element from the Christian Trinity was entirely bound up with the defeat of Gnosticism, as we shall presently see.

Trinitarianism regarding the Godhead was always known and taught by the initiates, even long prior to Christianity. For it is a universal principle, and what is more, it is an entirely logical outcome of the more fundamental teaching of monotheism. Thus its correct formulation, and the full understanding of its application, lay at the very heart of the Mystery wisdom. Early Christianity, knowing the Christ to be in a direct line of descent from the ancient Mysteries, inevitably grappled with this problem of the Trinity. Indeed, one can say that this issue lay at the very heart of all the heated Gnostic controversies in so far as it was the divine Sophia, that mediating Being of the Three who comprised the Trinity, who, as the archetypal feminine, was battling to have her rightful place in the emerging orthodoxy acknowledged, something which, as we have already seen, she patently failed to achieve.

ISIS, OSIRIS AND HORUS – THE EGYPTIAN TRINITY

It is therefore necessary to consider briefly this whole question of the Trinity in order to appreciate the sort of intellectual and spiritual milieu which formed the backdrop in which the young and purely Christian movement attempted to assert her independence over all other groups and cults actively seeking followers in The Gnosis.

The Trinitarian concept of the Godhead is complex and can be understood or studied on many different levels. We will try to simplify some of these before proceeding. The Trinity is, as we have said, directly related to monotheism. For, briefly stated, whether one views the problem philosophically, theologically, or even mathematically, once the essential unitary nature of God becomes recognized, and his Creation as being something substantially identical yet separately manifest, he must of necessity have had to draw something out of himself, i.e. the One must have become Two; and if these Two are not to be totally separated and moreover are to remain truly united, they must do so by virtue of a third, connecting principle. This is the most basic of all expressions of the idea or concept of the Three in One and the One in Three, the spiritual Trinity. From here it can take on the most varied of forms, but in the mythological traditions of the ancient Mysteries out of which Christianity developed it, its most popular, profound, and also most easily assimilated version is the well-known Egyptian Trinity of Isis, Osiris, and Horus. The primal consciousness of the Egyptians hovered around this mythological family of Father, Mother, and Son in the very same way as the Christian consciousness revolved or still revolves around the Holy Family.

While this is an obvious and fundamental analogy, it is, however, one whose Christian significance can only be understood if the relationship to the Egyptian model is properly elaborated, for in doing this we are able to gain an insight into the vanished spirit of Sophia. Thus, in the Christian theological Trinity, the feminine aspect of the Godhead is significantly almost non-existent, despite the fact that Sophia is nothing less than a Greek philosophical and conceptual development of the spiritual reality which, for the Egyptians, lay behind their Goddess Isis! We thus come to the real truth of the matter underlying the trinitarian controversies in the young Church.

The hard-headed theologians who gained eventual power over the Gnostics at this time, when the ancient Mystery connection with Christianity was still being energetically thrashed out, did so precisely because of their ability to theologize Sophia and her mystery *out* of the newly evolving Christian idea of the Trinity! She was simply eliminated or at best reduced to the status of a ghost, albeit a holy one! This is also the primary explanation why Christianity eventually became such an anaemic, legalistic, tradition-rooted, dogmatic, and male-dominated religion, far removed from the fresh, full-bodied, and spiritually infused movement it was intended to be by its Sophia-inspired initiator, and actually was at the beginning.

The modern spiritual demise of Christianity is directly related to all this. This is also the reason why Sophia, knowledge of whom has continued to be cultivated in Esoteric Christianity down the centuries, must be allowed back into mainstream Christian consciousness if Christianity is to become filled with the spirit once again as it was so abundantly in its beginnings.

BODY, SOUL AND SPIRIT – THE HUMAN TRINITY

Leaving aside this direct Sophia connection for a moment, if we are to attempt a genuine portrayal of the spiritual demise of the Church, we must, to begin with, also have a pretty clear idea of just what it is we are talking about when we use the word *spirit*. It is a word which, despite or even because of its common currency, is not easy to understand in its essence.

Let us therefore outline, for clarity's sake, a definition of this word. Hopefully our brief definition will allow its deeper meaning to unfold as the principal tenets of this book are developed and (again hopefully) are grasped by unprejudiced readers. For it will be seen that no true understanding of this word is possible at all, and thus no conceptual framework can ever truly evolve through which genuine spiritual knowledge can be fostered, unless or until the word *spirit* is properly grasped. This can be done only when spirit itself is considered within that framework which, as we have already indicated, lies at the very heart of all mystery wisdom and knowledge, i.e. the Trinitarian framework. Let us therefore examine this problem briefly with this in mind.

Every normal adult is aware of him or herself as being, or possessing, a physical body. This goes without saying! Most people, however, will also fairly readily acknowledge that they possess a soul as well, though this word has lost the clarity it once possessed in ascribing to man a purely spiritual, as distinct from a merely material or natural being. Thus, many people nowadays prefer to use the word 'mind' or even 'consciousness' instead of soul. Only a few will be able with any degree of certainty or articulation to espouse the possession of 'a spirit' or 'spirit'. Though the word 'spirit' itself, as we have already said, is widely used, and not just in relation to religious matters, the possession of it by an individual in the same concrete form as the body, or in the same easily identifiable aspect of mind or soul, is rarely admitted to, and if it is, even more rarely understood.

Without entering into the heady ontological complexities in which it is possible to indulge here, on a more down-to-earth level it can easily be seen that for modern man, the problem of the 'spirit' is largely conceptual[5]. To an earlier form of consciousness, however, even one as relatively recent as the early Christian consciousness, this was manifestly *not* the case. Then, man lived in a much closer proximity to his God or gods. This intimacy, however, did not prevent man from expressing his understanding of the relationship with his God or gods in a very profound manner. Quite the contrary: he was in fact capable of a very elaborate and erudite expression of it. Moreover, it was a relationship he always characterized in *trinitarian* terms, terms which in our modern language can easily be seen to correspond to body, soul, and spirit. Through a constant study of the manner in which this communion with their gods took place, the Initiates were also able to identify, in the most basic of its governing principles, how spiritual or indeed any kind of knowledge arises.

Moreover, they knew that the framework for expressing this spiritual/religious knowledge had of necessity to take a trinitarian form. The Initiates' entire knowledge, wisdom, and teaching was based firstly on their awareness of God as a divine *spirit*, secondly on their own separate physical presence as *body*, and thirdly on that which mediates between these two polar, yet directly connected spirit and physical realities, their own *soul*. And all three, they knew, were interconnected in the most intimate and complex ways.

This, briefly stated, indicates the methodology used in this book also. Thus it will be seen that an increasing clarity can and will prevail regarding the psychical aspect of religious matters generally if this method is rigorously adhered to. This method has the finest possible credentials and is indeed firmly rooted in the spiritual history of mankind itself, notwithstanding the fact that knowledge of it has been submerged by centuries of Sophia-starved intellectual wrangling, most of it between males.

The truth of what we are getting at here can be best illustrated and fully appreciated by looking at one of the greatest Initiates of all time, one who nevertheless enjoys the advantage of having lived within the fairly narrow limitations of our recorded Western history. This is the famous sage, Pythagoras.

PYTHAGORAS

Pythagoras (d. circa 500 B.C.) was one of the very earliest of the classical Greek philosophers. He acquired his renowned and vast wisdom in many ways, not the least of which was through a life of deep meditation and reflection. But he was also an extremely active person. Throughout his life he travelled extensively in the ancient world, absorbing, everywhere he went, the essence of the then-extant eastern Mystery teachings (or more precisely, what was left of them, for by then they were, for various reasons, very much in decline). He eventually settled in southern Italy and there he formed a Mystery centre.

Pythagoras was in many ways a transitional figure in that he represents a bridge between the old Mystery wisdom cultivated secretly in the temples from time immemorial and a new style of 'academic'[6] learning, which was much more openly practised. The latter phenomenon can be attributed to the Greeks who inaugurated it around this time. As such it was a new and vitally important departure for the human spirit, for it was an activity with the deepest and most far-reaching consequences for human evolution, which we have come to know simply as *philosophy*.

Pythagoras was at the forefront of this movement. He was thus in his teachings doing something quite extraordinary and revolutionary for his time: he was attempting to give conceptual expression to what formerly was taught in the Mysteries only in a pictorial way through myth, symbol and the like. He was thus one of the prime initiators of our modern civilization in that he set in motion what was to become in time one of our greatest assets, the art of pure conceptual thinking. Whereas formerly pictures, images, or indeed real visions of the gods and goddesses were the keys to unlocking the enigmas of spiritual, psychical, and physical reality, in Pythagoras's system all is reduced to *Nous*, *Thumos* and *Phrenes*, three Greek words which denote body, soul, and spirit.

Needless to say, Pythagoras's teaching was vast and his wisdom profound. His trinitarianism, however, we must note very carefully, is its most fundamental and basic characteristic. And though it is possible to piece together many of his teachings through Plato and others, this Mystery wisdom of Pythagoras was by and large either lost or discarded, or the books recording it were burnt, along with all the rest of the ancient wisdom teachings. This destruction was perpetrated by the proponents of orthodox Christianity who had finally defeated Gnosticism by the 4th century. It is a loss from which we still suffer! One of its most obvious and enduring effects is that it denies human beings access to the only true method which enables them to conceptualize or even see 'spirit.'

KNOW THYSELF

This loss of the ability to conceptualize 'spirit,' or rather more accurately, the historical process to which it has succumbed and which needs to be understood in order for it to be fully activated again in our own time, is part of the whole purpose of this book, through the reading of which hopefully a clearer understanding of the problem will emerge. Here however it is necessary to merely establish the fact that the trinitarianism invariably discernible at the heart of the ancient mystery religions was a wisdom and spirit-filled expression and recognition of how God images himself forth into the visible and physical world, and especially into the being of man himself. In the Mysteries, knowledge of God and knowledge of man were intimately linked together. The inscription 'KNOW THYSELF'[7] was always the key rule, the very password of the ancient temples, and this in itself indicates very clearly how the triune concept or image of God was the very same foundational framework for the initiates' image and knowledge of man and also of the world.

In the ancient initiation-knowledge, man in his deepest and truest image was always understood as not just a being comprised of a terrestrial body plus a soul which gives it consciousness and life, but also a divine spark of true *spirit*. Man was thus conceived of in his deepest sense as a cosmic being, a microcosmic replica of a macrocosmic reality, God. The universe itself was separated from neither God nor man. All three were reflections, to varying degrees of perfection, of one another, with the universal feminine soul as the grand and great cosmic mediator.

So with these primal thoughts in our mind regarding the fascinating but flickering mystery of the human/divine spirit, we will now begin to trace a) its marvellous igniting within the crucible of early Christianity; b) its almost complete snuffing out by the advance of orthodoxy; and c) its continuing glow within the hidden mantle of Esoteric Christianity.

CHAPTER THREE

A VESSEL IS PREPARED
IN THE EAST

———ooooOoooo———-

Christianity grew, as we have noted, out of the ancient Mystery knowledge, a tradition of cosmic wisdom practised from time immemorial in the secret sanctuaries and temples of the Initiates. This knowledge reached a very high point of sophistication in ancient Egypt, as even a cursory look at its religion and mythology will prove.

The influence of Egyptian mythology and theology on early Christianity is quite well established historically. But insofar as we are trying to define the unique spirit of early Christianity, this Egyptian influence can only be understood and fully appreciated when the nation or religion of Israel is seen as the link or bridge between these two cultures, i.e. between the very ancient culture of Egypt and the newly emerging culture of Christianity. In turn, we will be able to gain our best insight into this process when we understand the role played by the great prophet Moses.

As a priest of the Egyptian Mysteries of Osiris, Moses[8] had been initiated into the deepest and most sublime wisdom available to man in the then-civilized world. His destiny indeed marked him out as one of the greatest seers mankind has ever known, a destiny which he fulfilled primarily through his inspired application of the mystery principle of monotheism.

Through him this principle, hitherto concealed beneath the triple veil of the Mysteries, issued from the recesses of the temple and entered into the domain of history. Moses was bold enough to turn the loftiest principle of initiation into the sole dogma of a national religion, and yet so prudent that he revealed its consequences to none but a small number of initiates, imposing it on the masses by fear. In this the prophet of Sinai had evidently far-sighted views which looked beyond the destinies of his own people. The universal religion of mankind was the true mission of Israel, a mission few Jews, except their greatest Prophets have understood.[9]

Almost singlehandedly, Moses conceived of and hammered together, out of the nomadic tribes of Semites who were enslaved during his time in Egypt, a people and a nation capable and worthy of hosting an event as supremely significant for the whole of mankind as the Incarnation.

THE STORY OF MOSES

The fascinating and supremely heroic story of Moses can be pieced together chiefly from the Old Testament as well as other minor sources, all more or less historical. But the story of his conception and gestation of the Jewish nation, its fierce struggles for birth and survival in a hostile environment, and its eventual establishment and prosperity, all of which were due to his vast and wisdom-filled influence, is nothing if not archetypal. It is nothing if not a universal or epic depiction of the struggle of Everyman as he tries to make his way through the darkness of the material world with its manifold allurements, enticements, and deceptions, and towards the healing spirit-light of the pure vision of his God.

This great task filled Moses with not only a god-like zeal, but also a great sadness.

For what he saw, did, and heard during all the years of his momentous work, coupled with his initiated eye of seership which could stretch his vision forwards into the distant future – all of this gave to Moses enough insight into the flickering loyalties and passions of man to know how desperately his people needed the authority of the God he had revealed to them. He also needed to work constantly upon the inculcation of this authority if they were going to remain on the straight and narrow path, and fulfil the mission carved out for them by destiny. A great worry and sadness undoubtedly issued from such a vision, for when he was gone, when he was no longer with them in the flesh, what would become of these tribal people, his very own spiritual children? Who but himself was capable of wielding a rod as powerful, judicial, and wise as the one he possessed? It was indeed a burden of great dimension producing a sadness worthy of a god.

Just before he died, however, Moses received what was undeniably the most comforting of all his many spiritual revelations. For then there was made known to him a secret, a knowledge which seemed to his restless soul more subtle and sublime than that which he would possess if all the many pearls of wisdom he had yet acquired were rolled into one dazzling piece: in his old age Moses learned the great news from God that One was coming who would complete the magnificent work he had begun and into which he had poured the vast resources of his great soul and spirit. 'Then the Lord said to me, I will raise up for them a prophet like you, one of their own race and I will put my words into his mouth and he shall convey all my commands to them' (Deut. 18:17-18). This is precisely what Moses needed to know. He could thus die in peace knowing not only that his own work and the work of his nation would in time be fulfilled, but that the work of every man and woman on the face of the Earth was to become capable in time of its proper spiritual fulfilment, for in this revelation Moses had become prophetically aware of the future Incarnation of the Christ on Earth.

When this eventually came about some thirteen hundred years after the death of Moses, the concept of monotheism had been firmly and fully entrenched in the psyches of the Israelites. Moreover, it had become, as Moses well foresaw, the very lifeblood of the Jewish Nation as it struggled to retain its spiritual coherence and dignity in the face of great secular temptations, constant persecutions, and even wholesale captivity and enslavement. Monotheism nevertheless did manage to survive, and in doing so the crystal clear spiritual light of true religious idealism was kept alive in the world.

From the beginning Moses had laid down the Law of God for the Israelites with all the sternness of a caring father who struggles to bring dignity, purpose, and hope to a large family of wayward children who would otherwise be scattered upon the winds of worldly dissipation without ever achieving anything of worth in life. Thus, in their own very best interests, he made God the most important thing in their lives.

This God, Jehovah, was undoubtedly a stern God, one the people feared as well as respected. He was, however, largely perceived by the people as a male God, a father God, a bit, one could even say, like Moses himself! For if Moses was going to rule this unruly lot, he knew instinctively that he must utilize the masculine and forceful power of the purely male *spirit* as opposed to the much more gentle, feminine, and earthly orientated power of the *soul*.[10]

THE FATHER SPIRIT

This was surely a hard choice for him, but it was one he felt he had to make. And so the Trinitarian nature of the monotheistic Godhead, incorporating as well as spirit both the soul and the earthly Nature herself, barely figured in the Mosaic religion, for there was, as the Mosaic Law revealed, only *one* God and absolutely no other. It was a religion of the application of monotheism *par excellence*. As such it evoked only the Father spirit and it was his worship only that was imposed on the whole of the simple tribal people of Israel. Moses was applying, in an acutely singular fashion, the specifically *spiritual* power of his God which he nevertheless knew himself to be Trinitarian in nature. But he wished to establish on the firmest possible ground the presence on the Earth of this spirit with whom he communicated so intimately, even if it were the case that he should reveal only *one* aspect of the totality of its divinity. He had very specific and crystal clear reasons for doing this. He knew he was, via the Jewish Nation, preparing a vessel for nothing less than the incarnation of the divine Word itself. This Word had been prophetically revealed to him, and through its revelation he gained all his power, and it stood as the reason behind all his actions.

To the cosmic or astrologically determined consciousness of the wise ancients, including Moses, it was towards the Sun that they always looked when seeking the abode of this divine Word. The Sun was always regarded as the abode of the highest of all the ancient divinities. Here was a masculine Being *par excellence*. Here was a God who had been regarded from the very earliest civilizations, beginning from Vedic times in India onwards, as representing the magnificent and solar power of the divine Word and who, precisely because of this, was always conceived of and given expression to, in the most sublime, profound, and loftiest of terms.

It was this same divinity whom our early gnostic Christians called the Logos (meaning 'Word' in Greek), seeing in him the full Trinitarian revelation of the Godhead. It was indeed in this manner that the hope of Moses found its fulfilment in early Christianity.

THE SOLAR LOGOS

In attempting as we are here to behold the tangibility, the reality of the spirit of Esoteric Christianity, the role played by the heavenly body of the Sun should be carefully noted. There should be no misunderstanding here! We refer openly to the fact that this star, our Sun, had a direct spiritual bearing upon the genesis of Christianity, and represents the key to understanding the new-risen bodily nature of man, inaugurated at the first Easter.

Some people may find such a notion somewhat alarming or disturbing. However, this is usually only the case with those who consciously or (usually) unconsciously cut themselves off from a relationship with Nature beyond one of a most superficial kind. It is sadly a common condition nowadays, and one which can only be properly addressed by a conscious effort to reawaken or revitalize the relatively dormant senses of man. When this is properly done, and in a balanced fashion, the soul-filled reality of 'Mother Nature' soon awakens in the individual.

This kind of soul and Sun-filled thinking and feeling the early Christians willingly and enthusiastically practised and integrated fully into their new religion. Regarding their understanding of the overwhelming importance of the Sun specifically, this is something which is indeed very evident from the Gospel itself. The very opening sentence of the most profound, spiritual and esoteric of all the Gospels, St. John's, refers to this solar deity: 'In the beginning was the Word (Logos).'[11]

The ancient religions are renowned for their worship of the various planetary deities. Each tribe or grouping had, for whatever reasons, its own peculiar or particular favourites. As the aeons passed and mankind progressed, however, it was to the Sun more than any other heavenly body that man gradually turned to offer his purest sacrifices and perform his most instructive rites of worship. This was a slow yet inevitable turning, involving a multiplicity of factors, climatic and geographic as well as purely psychic and psychological.

Nevertheless, the Solar Logos has long figured in mankind's religious consciousness, for, beginning in India thousands of years before the rise of the great classical Egyptian civilizations, the universal power of the Sun and its God had already been well recognized.

KRISHNA

It was through the great Indian avatar Krishna at the very dawn of man's civilized life on earth, that a mighty revelation of God in his solar Logos aspect was first established.

> *Krishna reveals to men the idea of the divine Word; never more will they forget it. After Krishna, there passes a powerful radiation, so to speak, of the solar Word, through the temples of Asia, of Africa, and of Europe. In Persia we have Mithras, the reconciler of the luminous Ormuzd and of the sombre Ahriman; in Egypt Horus, son of Osiris and Isis; in Greece, Apollo, god of the Sun and of the lyre; Dionysus, who roused souls to life. Everywhere the solar god is a mediating god, and the light is also the word of life.*

It was by Krishna that this idea entered the ancient world; it is by Jesus that it is to shed its rays throughout the whole Earth. [12]

We have seen that Jesus enters the world through the Judaic nation and its religion. If we then try to relate all of this to the still later and gradual emergence of the specific spirit of Christianity, we must do so by asking: How can we identify precisely the way in which this Solar Logos power enters the Judaic stream of wisdom?

For an answer, we must turn to Moses once more.

It is through him that we can observe this solar power strongly at work, for in the manner in which he received his mighty and far-reaching spiritual revelations can be seen the unmistakable drawing nearer and nearer to the Earth of this Sun spirit, a process which culminated eventually in the Incarnation itself. Perhaps the famous incident of the Burning Bush in the Old Testament is the best illustration of this. In this scene from the Book of Exodus (Chapter 3), God appears to Moses as fire or an unquenchable flame. To the all-embracing spirit and cosmic consciousness of Moses, a flame which spoke spirit revelations of the mightiest kind could be nothing if not the reflected microcosmic image of the real and macrocosmic Sun God!

When this Spirit reveals to the perplexed Moses that his (God's) name is I AM, we can see foreshadowed in this highly instructive Old Testament episode the essence of what was later understood by the first Christians as the 'Word becoming flesh' in the Incarnation. The Incarnation was or is conceived of as being nothing less than that spiritual/historical event by which each and every individual human being became empowered to recognize in himself, in his or her very own flesh and blood, the reality of an in-dwelling God. In other words, the Incarnation empowers us through our I AM centre to be able to participate in the Being of God. This is the reason the God of the Old Testament speaks thus.

This crystal clear and pure knowledge of the Sun or Solar Logos nature of the Christ was very alive in the early Church, as the most esoterically significant of the Gospels (St. John's) proves.[13] For the relationship of the Sun and the Father aspect of the Godhead was still very clear in the minds of these early Christian initiates, due principally no doubt to the Mosaic Mystery tradition.

In highlighting the Sun nature of Christ's divinity, insofar as the solar God and the divine Word were seen as synonymous, the whole question of just who Christ was, was thus brought entirely into focus, if not absolute resolution, in the early Church. In the early Christian consciousness, the fact that the solar light becomes identified with divine light, or 'enlightenment', is not in truth very difficult to understand. For, given that they possessed a less abstract form of consciousness than our own – a consciousness which was still very much coloured by a spiritual wisdom which saw far more than a mere ball of fire in the sky when it beheld the Sun – it is entirely to be expected that they would have been able to see in the teaching, in the very being of Christ, if not the actual Sun, then a reflection of its rays, for they experienced through him a light which gave to them a spiritual clarity of consciousness far greater than any they had yet experienced.

These early and highly learned initiates and

philosophers who meditated deeply upon the Incarnation found in it nothing less than *the* most significant contribution ever made to the overall development of human consciousness. They could indeed envision the spiritual implications of this great event of the Incarnation and its universality as plainly as they beheld the very Sun in the sky! The concept of the divine Logos, as they came to see it in its embodiment in the Incarnation, carried or carries the whole process of the development of human consciousness a huge step further along its proper evolutionary path by injecting into it a new and mighty soul/spiritual impulse! Thus, their faith, their knowledge, and especially their spiritual vision could allow them to indeed 'see' the very Word incarnate.

THE LIVING WORD

The Word, however, it must be said, is always, in the early Christian consciousness, the spiritual and Living Word and never the merely mechanical or abstract one to which we are accustomed. Thus we can understand how and why Christ is seen in St. John's Gospel as both the living or divine Logos and also the Word made flesh.

Herein we can grasp the kernel, and feel the whole heat of the debates that raged about Christ and his origins within The Gnosis. Back then (as indeed is still the case now), very direct questions were continually being asked that needed equally direct answers: Who was he? Where did he come from? By whose authority does he speak? etc. Unlike nowadays, however, when we have so many other things to distract our minds, these were the very hottest topics of the day during The Gnosis, and, it should be noted, not just for philosophers and theologians, but for everyone. The canonical Gospels, and especially John's, indicate clearly this perplexity about Jesus, but do so mainly on behalf of the Jews. But the Gospels, it must be remembered, are as much *archetypal* as they are historical, and the Jews' questions in this sense merely represent questions that everyone had, and still has, the right to ask. In The Gnosis these questions constituted the pervading spiritual atmosphere. Everyone then suddenly felt, given the very nature of the Incarnation, that they had the authority to talk about spiritual matters, speak up, and throw in their tuppenceworth! Some, because they were bold and daring enough, even went on to develop their own, often idiosyncratic versions of the Gospel.

Today, we can barely sense the subtleties and intensity of these controversies that raged in and around Palestine at this time! Given the small number of relevant documents that have survived, and also taking into account the breadth and depth of wisdom that is lost through translation (from the Greek mainly), we merely get a faint hint, through even the best exegesis, of just what was going on in the minds and hearts of the people at this time and place.

However, all of these controversies regarding Christ, his origin and so on eventually somehow got hammered out and into the early theological concept of the Christian Trinity. What is more pertinent, however, from the point of view of our present study is that the eventual formulation of this still current Christian Trinity is utterly tied up with the expedient means by which Gnosticism was finally defeated within the orthodox Church. The intellectual sharpness of the Christian Trinity was achieved at the expense of the central yet expansive Sophia mystery which represented the hallmark, nay, the very essence of Gnosticism. This loss to the Church of the generous and all-embracing Sophia wisdom also indicted clearly why Christian theologians invariably get the Logos and the Sophia concepts, as aspects of the Godhead (a knowledge that was so important, exact, and alive in early Christianity), very mixed up! Philosophical clarity will only prevail when correspondences are sought and found between these Greek concepts in the Gospel and the lost Trinitarian mystery wisdom.

THE INCARNATION

This is a work, however, which calls upon and evokes the substantial spirit of Esoteric Christianity through which true knowledge of the Sophia-Christ has been, and still is, kept alive in the world. We shall later follow the fascinating vicissitudes of this spirit in the outer history of the Church. Though it is a fact that we must regard it as esoteric, this spirit, and the wisdom and knowledge it bestows, has nevertheless managed to survive in the world, due no doubt to its own great inner power and resilience. Its cultivation gives living, genuine, and vibrant insight into not only the Sun origin and the mysterious significance of the Christ Being himself, but it also reveals the Incarnation in its most profound and occult/spiritual depths. In doing this it draws out of the Incarnation it's unique I AM nature, and gives to the student a sensation, if not a tangible vision, of the reality of Christ's Presence in the world. In this, of course, lies, and indeed has always lain in the Church, the very keynote of the Incarnation's significance, whether esoteric or exoteric.

****

It was the perceived *uniqueness* of the Incarnation which had set men's spiritual aspirations aflame in Palestine at the beginning of our era. This religious fervour took place not only in the first couple of centuries after the Incarnation's actual occurrence, but also, and very revealingly, in the century or so before it, too. An event with such implications for the whole future of mankind as the Incarnation can justifiably lay claim to be, indeed must of its very nature be capable of sending via the medium of the Earth's finer substances to those capable of receiving them, currents of its foreknowledge. Thus it was that wise men, soothsayers, sensitives, and inspired clairvoyants of greatly diverse character, religious background and spiritual training could not but divine something of its impending import. Through their extrasensory faculties or sciences of divination, they could not but determine that some happening, if not *the* most decisive event ever to take place in the history of mankind, was approaching, or indeed had actually occurred!

All of this activity was quite apart from the solid and orthodox prophetic tradition of Israel itself which had for many centuries been predicting the advent of One whom it saw as not only its own Saviour but also the Suffering Servant of all mankind. Thus it can be seen that in this unique Event of the Incarnation there is embodied the culmination of the esoteric and messianic thread of hope ran not only through the whole of the Jewish tradition from Moses onwards, but that also encapsulates the deepest spiritual aspirations and intuitions of men and women everywhere.

CHAPTER FOUR

THE REJECTION OF SOPHIA

The Incarnation lays claim to uniqueness on many different levels! No one with even a little knowledge of it can deny this! What we are here endeavouring to establish, however, are those tenets within it, knowledge of which must be cultivated if its perceived uniqueness is to be integrated into human consciousness in its full spiritual richness. This was, after all, the very process which constituted the chief dynamic of what we may call the Gnostic Church before this great effort was so tragically snuffed out. It is, however, a process that can and indeed must be revived if those who deeply care about Christianity wish it to be renewed in the way that many long for.

But this in its turn can only begin if and when the Incarnation is seen in its true and proper perspective and in its most instructive character, which is as a continuation of the ancient mystery/wisdom tradition, albeit in a modern form.

When the early Christians began to first organize themselves into groups on a large scale, the divorce, referred to earlier, from the ancient Sophia-inspired mystery wisdom certainly allowed the body of the Church to establish itself as the entirely new spiritual and religious entity which it could validly lay claim to be, insofar as it placed the Event of the Incarnation at the centre of all its teachings. It wanted, and rightly so, to establish itself as something totally new and different from all other cults contemporary with it, and it attempted to do this on many different levels, intellectual as well as practical.

But in the most important aspect of this work, in the formation of that primary image without which no religion can exist at all, i.e. its image of God, the Church made its biggest mistake (to date!). In creating on the one hand a purely theological and entirely male-orientated trinitarian God-image, and then in compensation for the obvious feminine deficiency within this image and (merely as a kind of afterthought) promoting a Marian cult quite separate from the Godhead, the Church could not but cause a split within its spiritual consciousness. In other words, if its image of its worshipful God (an image which should, after all, by Biblical definition contain the *whole* of man's existential experience)[14] effectively excluded at least half of this experience (the female half!), how could this God not but cause a split in man's spiritual consciousness? However, if the Church was to incorporate properly the feminine element into its image of the Godhead, it should not have broken its connection with the ancient Mysteries in the manner in which it did! For this wholeness in both the image of God and its temporally reflected reality in the Church's body, was something which ideally could and still can be achieved only through a properly constituted and holistically disseminated trinitarianism, as understood from time immemorial by the Initiates.

As the Church evolved however, there came, as a result of the defeat of Gnosticism and the rejection of knowledge *per se* that this very defeat implies, a total splitting off of the knowledge of God from the reality of the Church's day-to-day existence. And it could or can be no other way! For unless this mystery *knowledge* of God (gnosis) and the manner of its correct dissemination is understood, something quite different from the promotion of a blind *faith* in God, the Church must remain truncated, even headless, groping in the dark for that shining light at its centre, the spirit-mystery of its founder!

JESUS: A NEW KIND OF HUMAN BEING

The very early Gnostic Church gained its individuality and much of its vitality precisely because it had possessed this wholeness of spiritual perception and vision. These early saints and followers of the new Way could conceive of Christ not only as a human representative of the Father spirit whom Jesus's ancestors, the Jews, had for so long worshipped; they could also behold in him something entirely new, health-giving, and spiritually uplifting, an almost unfathomable quality they had never witnessed in anyone or anywhere before. He was quite simply a totally different kind of human being. Everything he did and said

– from the manner of his dealing with the religious customs and conventions of his time, to his attitude towards children, but most especially in his relationship with women – all these spoke tremendously of his great difference from his contemporaries. The reason he could be so shockingly 'loose' in his behaviour was because he had been able, with angelic complicity, to incorporate fully into his being the feminine aspect of the Godhead, which had been largely unknown to the Jews. The Sophia spirit was, and is, of the very essence of enlightenment, and though he speaks, through the Gospels, of the Father in much more overt tones (for this Father God, was, strictly speaking, the only one the Jews knew about!), Christ's knowledge of the Sophia spirit was not questioned by the Gospel's writers.

Apart from many of the Sophia-inspired, apocryphal writings of the period, our familiar canonical Gospels also indicate this awareness in various ways. For instance, in the early Church, where the use of symbol was both highly selective and vitally significant, the *dove*, representing the culmination or completion of Jesus's spiritual initiation, is the most precise indication possible of his intimacy with the Divine Feminine, for the dove was always that by which the ancient mystery wisdom indicated the soul or feminine aspect of the trinitarian Godhead. Moreover, it will be remembered that it was the spirit, in the form of a (white) dove, who descended upon Jesus at his baptism by John in the Jordan just before he (Jesus of Nazareth) began his momentous three years' ministration of this spirit on the Earth and in the flesh.

Once the unique nature of Christ as the very Word incarnate began to circulate in Palestine in the aftermath of the Incarnation, there began inevitably to group around this revelation men and women from all kinds of backgrounds and cultures and of every degree of initiation, wisdom, and knowledge, or even of none at all. Nevertheless, it was of course the learned ones who possessed the capabilities of giving direction to this great new spiritual movement.

And many of these people were thoroughly acquainted with, if not actual initiates of, the ancient Mystery teachings.

It should be noted that the term 'initiate' by this time did not have the same weight as it would have had in similar circles at a time when the Mysteries were much purer in their spiritual content and were not as diluted as they had become by the beginning of our era. Indeed, by Jesus' time pagan initiation had taken on as much the philistine attraction of political expediency as it had of spiritual enlightenment! Nevertheless, the knowledge possessed by the early Christians who had converted from the older Mysteries was vital to the formation of the new young Church's vibrant spiritual content.[15]

THE DELICATE MAGIC OF THE EARLY CHURCH

Thus the magic of the early Gnostic Church was very much to do with its infusion by a tradition and a trinitarianism almost as old as mankind itself. It was a tradition possessed of a wisdom of infinite depth, coherence, and beauty, based on a precise, even mathematical cosmology, which knew at first-hand the spiritual entities which originated and animated every single body in the universe, from the

Initiate's own, to the Earth itself, and to the ones, magnificent beyond all imagining, revolving in the heavens.

Of course, it was a gigantic task the Church had here in trying to bring all of this to bear upon the Incarnation, not least because the Mystery traditions had by this time almost vanished anyway! It was merely echoes of this wisdom that were resounding in the early Christian movement. The most astute of the Christian converts nevertheless knew at least the essence of these traditions of which the Trinitarian concept of the Godhead, inclusive of the feminine, was primary.

Despite the fact that these enlightened people were usually anathematized by orthodoxy in the end, it was nonetheless their work and effort that ensured the injection of the pure spirit into the Church in the first place. And the survival of this spirit, even in its very anaemic manifestation nowadays, continues to rely to some extent upon them!

The Gnostic's key to spiritual knowledge lay in their understanding of the principle and power of initiation. For these early Christian initiates, what was most remarkable of all about the Incarnation was that it had achieved something on the broad stage of human history that had previously been capable of achievement and permissible only within the highly secretive confines of the initiation temples. In the ancient Mysteries, the neophyte or initiand (i.e. one who is to be initiated) always received his initiation and his deepest spiritual inspirations in a more or less out-of-body state through a direct contact, via the soul, with the divinity, who afterwards always withdrew from him. The new initiate could then go out into the wider world once more and duly impart, in correct measure, to his flock, what he had mystically learned. In that spiritual event which came in time to be called the Incarnation, however, something entirely new was perceived to have entered into the whole process. The divinity came to be regarded as having descended directly, via John's baptism, into one Jesus of Nazareth, one held to be human by all means, but one who had also possessed the astounding capability of hosting the divinity in such a manner that it could remain with him fully consciously, and moreover go with him in the fullest physical sense out into the world, passing with him even through the portal of death!

Such a thing was unheard of in the Mysteries before Jesus. Apart from anything else, the very idea of a god dying was totally and utterly new. For, it was neither thought possible nor necessary for this ever to happen. In the divine sacrifice, however, which constituted the most fundamental aspect of the Incarnation, it became increasingly obvious that this was the extraordinary way, indeed the *only way* in which man himself could ever now progress and hope to be raised to greater heights, even to godhood, in the future.

The physical as well as the spiritual consequences of this Event were thus seen to be of the most extraordinary and miraculous nature. Not only that, but the whole initiation process was thereby seen to have moved to any entirely new level, in that the personality, even the very physical body itself, was given an emphasis it never had or needed before in initiation rites and practices. It was the outwardness, even the historicity of the whole process of gaining or perceiving the spirit that was now being emphasized which gave initiation a completely new dimension compared to the former method of absolute inwardness and secrecy practised in the confines of the old temples.

Something of universal importance, something which had a direct relevance to every human being of whatever race, religion, colour, or creed was thus seen to have occurred. For initiation was now conceived of as being accessible to everyone and not just to a chosen few, as had always been the case in the past. *Now*, it was perceived, everyone could have 'gnosis', could know God for themselves. This was the real secret of the Incarnation. And when the word of it spread, inevitably spiritual turmoil was the result!

THE CHURCH TOUGHENS UP!

Indeed, that this turmoil was the primary feature of The Gnosis is very well known! It was also, however, that very same feature of the times which impelled the growing Christian Church into a spurning of Gnosticism. Although the early Christian Fathers may have been aware, in varying degrees of initiation, of just how the Incarnation was an inevitable outcome and development of the ancient Mystery tradition, they could also see that if the Church did not become properly constituted, in a temporal way at least, it had no hope of surviving, spiritually or otherwise, as an institutionalized force in the outer world, something which they felt it should accomplish. It was while in the process of achieving this latter purely temporal goal, however, that the Mystery knowledge eventually became totally separated from the established Church, and in time almost entirely lost to it as a vital and spiritually nourishing force.

Thus, although it is easy to ascertain that in the Gnostic Church there was a widespread acceptance of the fact that the Incarnation Event constituted a grand renewal of the Mystery tradition, it also must be accepted that this awareness gradually and sadly diminished as time went on. Rather than elaborating and clarifying the implications of this manifold connection with the ancient wisdom, so that it could foster a rich spiritual consciousness within its congregations, the Church developed into a dogmatic and theocratic institution. In many respects it merely reinstated, with a slightly altered constitution, the exoteric aspect of the old law-ridden Mosaic religion.

From the defeat of Gnosticism onwards, what constituted the spiritual element in the Church took on a very different guise. Spirituality was split off from the mainstream activity of the Church and gradually became merely a sort of side-lined branch of it. In time, it proved to be nothing less than a breeding ground for all kinds of strange activities, for the cultivation of what someone once called 'mystic mud'; and it was a splitting that also proved a sure-fire strategy for the eventual establishment of mere superstition as the only real 'spiritual' element in the lives of many ordinary folk. The great catastrophe was that eventually those who pursued knowledge of the true Mystery spirit became objects of fear, suspicion, and more often than not, outright hatred, a phenomenon of which the primary dynamics of medieval history gives us ample testimony.

The true spirit of God in man, of course, cannot ever be extirpated. This is especially the case from the time it achieved its unique and powerful uplift via the Event of the Incarnation. The existence of Esoteric Christianity is proof of this.

CHAPTER FIVE

THE FORGING OF AN ORTHODOXY

——ooooOoooo——

In our own day, history, in a spiritual sense, is actually repeating itself, for it is obvious that a grassroots change in attitude is afoot regarding the spirit and spirituality generally. The very deepest of questions are stirring within the hearts and souls of growing numbers of people from all walks of life, and matters pertaining to the soul and spirit-being of man are increasingly felt to be central to the proper resolution of so many of our modern world's ills. However dimly, inarticulately, or naively it might sometimes be felt or expressed, there is nevertheless a real and perceptible movement towards a resurrection or re-definition of this body of sublime wisdom and knowledge with which the ancients were so familiar.

The growing interest in early Celtic spirituality is one such sign, and perhaps the most potentially promising. Following fast on the heels of the upsurge of interest in all things Celtic, the early Celtic Church itself is gradually being discerned as having been infused with some vibrant, almost magical power which in a very short space of time transformed the existing pagan Celtic culture of old Hibernia into a new, vital and Christianized force.

For it is becoming increasingly obvious to historians, academics and others that that which lived in the ancient soul of Ireland and which had, through the power of the Incarnation, become infused and invigorated with a mighty new spiritual impulse, provided the chief foundation upon which the light of learning and civilization generally was kept alive in Europe at a time of ever-increasing chaos and darkness.

We have been indicating hitherto briefly and in general terms the reasons for this cultural decline in the early centuries of our era. These can be summarized and simplified by highlighting the defeat of the ancient light-filled esoteric knowledge in the East by the 4th century, as well as the growing barbarian invasions which caused chaos and the eventual break-up of the Roman Empire. There were also, of course, other, less obvious factors.

But it was a confluence of all of these adverse conditions that constituted the chief grounds for the development of a hard-headed and repressive Roman Catholic orthodoxy which, as the centuries passed, became ever more authoritarian, dogmatic, and militant. And the end result of all this was a slow but sure sinking of Western civilization into a social stew of superstition, intellectual dogmatism, and spiritual darkness, i.e. into what used to be called the Dark Ages.

THE MAGIC OF IRELAND

From time immemorial, however, the island of Ireland was known to possess a strange, magical, and light-filled quality, so much so that even the hard and matter-of-fact consciousness of the Roman Emperors and their cohorts always hesitated when they thought of hauling this mysterious outpost into their Empire. The result was that the Romans never darkened the doors of old Hibernia, which was thereby left to its own cocooned but spiritually productive mystical destiny. This most surely was the work of a benign Providence!

In this way the soul of the country remained, as far as the ancient wisdom was concerned, pure and relatively undisturbed, and the force of the Roman 'grid' with its legalistic and attendant militarism was never allowed to blemish it. It was as if a garden was being preserved, by a wise working of Providence, in which the seed-Word of the Gospel could find some genuinely fertile soil. For the Hiberno-Celtic soul was one that had been thoroughly suffused, perhaps more than any other folk-soul, with the sublime fragrance of the ancient wisdom, so much so that the land of Erin had acquired in ancient stories and legends the reputation of being nothing less than a piece of Paradise itself! It can thus be imagined how this island had become by the time of Christ a well-formed vessel into which the new outpouring of the spirit into the world, through the advent of the Incarnation, could flow. When this began to happen, it was duly received there and integrated into the soul of the nation with a powerful strength and grace. In this way, the Incarnation imparted to the soul and spirit of the people of Erin a resilience and a quality of endurance unmatched in its purity. Indeed, many sense this Hibernian spirit even in our own day as still possessing something of its original grace and magical essence.

A great spiritual search is in progress! And one of the most instructive and revealing aspects of this search, especially as it relates to Esoteric Christianity, is how it teaches the seeker to observe this spirit to have been so vibrantly alive and thriving within cultures and traditions so totally different for one another as the ancient Celtic one was from the ancient Palestinian! Moreover, it is this very universality that offers the promise that this spirit of true love and cosmic wisdom can be revived once more in our own time.

The same all-inclusive spirit of the Incarnation that can be seen to be at work here in the Irish soul in the 5th to the 8th centuries was also at work in the Eastern Gnosis, a few centuries earlier.

Though obviously having its prehistory in, and being nurtured and elaborated through the influence of the purely Eastern Mystery wisdom-traditions, this incarnational spirit however took an incredibly strong root in the fertile ground of the Celtic soul of the Irish.

The forces inherent in the Western hemisphere are, generally speaking, always of a harder, rougher, or earthier nature in contrast to the 'ethereal' East. It can thus be said that this incarnational spirit underwent a strengthening in its journey from the East into the Western Celtic consciousness. Here in this 'Emerald Isle' of Ireland it germinated, grew and blossomed at a time when it had been well-nigh obliterated in the East. Furthermore, one can see how this spirit even took on a more formed life in the Celtic West. For after its initial incubation in the East where it had shone gloriously for a couple of centuries, it is nevertheless seen by the 4th century to have almost completely wilted away there under the influence of an alien power. This was the power which had been concentrating in and around the military might of Rome, and which had been developing for many centuries, even prior to the Incarnation It was this self-same power which was set to become the foundation of the future Church's Western orthodoxy.

We will in Chapter Seven be looking much more closely at this aspect of our spiritual history and the vital part played by the Celtic Church, which set the stage and even defined the content of our current orthodoxy. Now, however, we must shift our focus somewhat.

SAUL OF TARSUS

In order to gain some little understanding of the complex web of forces at work in this forging of an orthodoxy, we need to look closely at the Mystery nature of a hugely important post-incarnational event in the East. This was a pivotal event, as a result of which what was eventually to become the aforementioned Roman Western orthodoxy managed to establish itself in the first place. The manner in which this shift towards the West took place is, though quite paradoxical, very revealing both as to how the Church became established, and also how it in effect came to reject the spiritual core of its true mission in the process.

What we will look at now, therefore, in order to illustrate this, is the famous and dramatic conversion to Christianity of one of its greatest initial opponents and antagonists, one Saul of Tarsus, later to be known as St. Paul.

Apart from Christ himself, it is to this particular individual that the Western Church looks as the supreme elucidator of its spiritual mission and purpose in the world.

It is hardly necessary to recount here the details of St. Paul's initiation into the Mystery nature of Christ[16], for it is an event that has in the course of time taken on an archetypal dimension, something which nevertheless does nothing to diminish the impact and implications of its purely *historic* actuality. We will, however, outline its essential features in an attempt to highlight its importance as the key transitional event which cleared the way for the new spirit-light of the Incarnation to radiate outwards from its cocooned or chrysalis-like beginnings in Palestine and into the world in its full colour, brightness and purity, unimpeded by any kind of antiquated or inhibiting customs and rites. These indeed posed a great initial danger to the radiant power of the Incarnation, given the strength of the tradition and culture in which it was enacted, and by virtue of which the very 'chrysalis' was in the first place able to form.

Let us imagine this impeccably Jewish Saul riding high on his horse one day towards the town of Damascus, carrying with him the legal instruments necessary to eliminate as many as possible of what he saw as the absurd and highly disruptive Christian sect which had recently arisen in Judaism and had been fast gaining converts from the orthodox faith. We must remember that his was a very deep and powerful faith, the observance of which Saul meticulously kept, and whose customs, beliefs and legalities he was totally dedicated to upholding, down to the last jot and tittle. Saul, a man of highest possible standing and learning within his long, proud, and deeply religious culture, was no doubt infuriated by these weirdoes in Damascus, and gladly accepted the work of getting rid of them there, or anywhere else, for that matter! For they were teaching what sounded to him like absolute blasphemies, and were saying things and evolving practices which seemed, apart from penetrating right to the very heart of all that he held most zealously to be true about God and the world, nothing but the most malignant type of nonsense. They were spreading stories abroad which, although they claimed them to be the absolute truth, must, to any sensible person, be nothing but the purest of pure fiction! And fiction was something Saul had very little time for at all, whatever form it took! For he was, true to the finest qualities of his forebears, a man, in all matters, concerned only with the purest fact, and this was most especially the case when it came to matters concerning God and his holy Law. What these people were spreading abroad simply couldn't be true! That the one they claimed as their God, a mere carpenter from Nazareth by all accounts, had actually arisen from the dead, indeed! What absolute and utter gibberish! He, Saul, was going to make plain to them the real truth and was, in no uncertain terms, going to put them straight about religion, resurrection, God, Holy Writ, and especially the Law of Moses!

Providence, however, as it often does in even the most

meticulously laid plans, intervened. Saul's fearsome will and determination was to be transformed and redirected towards, for him, the most unlikely and unexpected of goals.

The duration or outwardly visible signs of the actual conversion or initiation experience of Paul, when he was struck from his high horse by a blinding light accompanied by other phenomena, should be of little consequence to anyone who is trying to assess it from the purely *spiritual* point of view. What should only matter from this point of view is the actual *inner* content of these experiences.

And it is this inner content we shall look at here, however tentatively. It has to be tentative, for by their very nature spiritual or religious experiences can be extraordinarily subtle as well as being, of course, deeply meaningful for the individual concerned. As such, they do not yield themselves to easy or generalized interpretation.

However, in this special case of St. Paul's we have an experience which is particularly significant and instructive. For as well as its undoubted impact upon Paul himself, it was also one which was to have the most profound influence on the whole future development of Western society. This single episode in the New Testament in truth represents the very fulcrum through which the Christian faith becomes established in its own right in the wider world, and not merely as another sect within Judaism, something which it was in danger if not actually in the process of becoming. This is a view widely accepted by Christian historians of all types regarding Paul and his initiation.

Thus, that Paul's conversion was of a most extraordinary nature there can be no doubt at all! At the same time, it must be pointed out that Paul's is only one, albeit the best known, of a great variety of extraordinary events indicated in the New Testament, relating to the manner in which growing numbers of people of all types and classes of greatly varied backgrounds, cultures and temperaments, were drawn to the Christ soon after the first Easter Sunday morning. People everywhere were being moved to the very depths of their being by the news of the Incarnation. And more than anything else it was the *individualized* aspect of the way in which the Incarnation initiation began to work in the world that was its most significant and essential characteristic. It had the power to touch and influence people in the most extraordinary and diverse ways.

ST. PAUL'S INITIATION

In ascertaining the spiritual importance of St. Paul's initiatory experience, however, we must be aware that it was of such an order that not only did it have the effect of instilling within him the great power necessary for laying the foundations of the new Church, something which, a few years after he had fully assimilated the experience, he set about doing with an almost superhuman zeal and energy; but his experience also gave him the inspiration necessary to communicate vitally through his inspired writings something of the real spiritual essence of Christ to peoples as greatly differing in soul and character as we are, say, from people of one or two thousand years ago, or as different in temperament and manners as, say, modern Chinese are from the Irish. To vast numbers and types of people, Paul's letters appear as fresh, subtle and as alive today as when they were first written nearly 2000 years ago!

It is obvious therefore that Paul has much to teach us regarding the true nature of the Christ and that furthermore he must be given very careful consideration in any study such as we are undertaking here. What we must first be quite clear about is that Paul's experience on the road to Damascus was nothing less than a true initiation, in the deepest possible meaning of this ancient term. It was a genuine initiation into the Mystery of Christ. He gives us a real hint as to how this spiritual event took place in his soul and body in those places in his writings where he refers to this new Mystery. This is something which he does most openly and directly in his famous letter to the Colossians. We thus may come to understand that Paul's 'secret' can be nothing less than an absolute initiatory certainty that his God had shaken off his own ancient and tightly guarded Mystery nature, emerged from the Holy of Holies of the Temple, and had incarnated into the wider earthly world! Not only that, but Paul could see that his God, whom he had up to this point known only in a predominantly intellectual, faithful, mystical, or some other more or less abstract way, had assumed a living and vibrant form, an immanent Presence in the world through none other than this very Jesus that he (Paul) had been, up to then, so totally dismissive of!

It was a most extraordinary and shattering realization! For he could now clearly see, and this is evident not necessarily from his account of his initiation, but from his writings generally, that this Jesus Christ had been able to miraculously unite himself with what we may call the bio-etheric stuff of the Earth itself, and moreover, that he did this in such an all-embracing fashion that it was no longer possible to truly know one's own physical self in one's ordinary awake consciousness without acknowledging the astonishing fact that, in one's deepest conscious essence, one had become identical with this Christ!

That Paul experienced all of this can be, without question, deduced from his writings, which are quite literally saturated with the spirit of Christ. For, coming to the fullest possible realization of this Sun-filled transformation of the Earth, meant also for Paul that his very own inner being itself underwent a veritable transfiguration. From then on it is evident he could no longer conceive of his own or indeed any mortal or earthly body in any other way than that of a living temple of the Christ Being. It was *the* most astonishing revelation possible for Saul and one we can share with him through his many letters in the New Testament, the study of which are necessary to any full and thoroughly modern Christian initiation.

Thus, on the road to Damascus we can say that the powerful monotheistic spirit of Paul's noble race, a spirit which in-dwelt and motivated him so single-mindedly and zealously, was in fact Christened through him! Prior to his initiation, the Incarnation was something Paul simply could not believe, for he had no reason to. Through his initiation experience, however, his spiritual faculties were opened and activated in such a way that no amount of reasoning power, no law, dogma, or ancient doctrines, however much he believed in them, could deny the reality of what he now beheld. This Jesus Christ was indeed alive! He had seen him, spoken to him, touched him! He was in everything, even in the food one ate! There was absolutely no doubt whatsoever about his living, his life-giving Presence, however extraordinary this may have seemed.

There are with regard to Paul's initiation both parallels with the ancient Mystery initiations as well as radical departures from them, which mark out Paul's as one in which a most remarkable transition took place. On the one hand, when we examine it in the light of the ancient Mysteries, it can be seen that there were compressed into this dramatic incident of Saul's conversion the principal features of all classic initiations where the disciple is led to the God through a death, or out-of-body experience, and then, some time later, returns or is 'reborn' again as a totally new man. This was the universal standard of initiation in the old temples, and always one of the most significant outcomes of it was that afterwards the disciple could no longer conceive of himself in the manner in which ordinary mortals conceive of themselves and their moral relationship to the world. The new initiate's experiences then were such that all matters concerning faith, beliefs and dogmas, all rules and regulations of whatever kind were simply swept aside, their usefulness having now been organically outgrown by the power and privilege bestowed on the disciple by the actual initiation itself. This can easily be intellectually comprehended. For at the point of initiation the disciple no longer merely believes or knows. He truly *sees*. He has active gnosis, *per se*. His prior, merely intellectual knowing, which he acquired as a neophyte, has now become actual spiritual seeing! And in achieving this full degree of initiation, God duly bestows his own immortality upon him. In this way the old mortal Saul became the reborn spirit-filled and renamed Christian Initiate, Paul.

CHRIST IS IN YOU!

Apart, however, from these classic similarities to older forms of initiation, Paul's experience is different in many respects. The most obvious of these is the manner in which he was able to achieve, through his initiation, the knowledge and awareness that not only did God, through the Christ Being, take absolute possession of his own (Paul's) soul and spirit, but this spirit took possession of his *body*, too. Moreover, he saw that this was also something which, to an equal or lesser degree, could now apply to everyone under the Sun! Thus, when Paul reveals his 'secret' to the Colossians that 'Christ is in you,' he literally means, and is absolutely certain of, precisely that! All of his instructions, admonitions, prayers, and blessings throughout his letters in the New Testament are inspired attempts to encourage his congregations to awaken to this awesome yet wonderful reality. Christ has done an immense spiritual Deed for you, was Paul's basic message. Now you yourself must do the rest.

As he tried to indicate in accordance with his own initiation, it was as if a spiritual lightening flash had impregnated the entire physical universe and everything in it now possessed the possibility of a divine renewal through the Incarnation.

And so it was in this way that a consciousness of the global Church of Christ began to awaken, first in Paul, and then in the hearts and souls of Christ's first followers.

Through his tireless missionary journeys, his sermons, talks, and especially for us, his letters, Paul set the tone of this new movement and tuned its pitch to the highest possible spiritual and moral standards.

It was in this way that early Christian orthodoxy, as a power in its own right, independent of the Judaism in which it was conceived and gestated, arose directly out of Paul's initiatives, which in turn were born *in toto* out of his all-embracing Damascus *initiation*. The later, highly dogmatic Christian orthodoxy that superseded Paul's early free spiritual one was not of his making. The emergence of this later Roman Catholic orthodoxy can be traced directly back to the fact that the link with the ancient Mystery knowledge was conveniently forgotten or indeed totally severed, posing as it did in its Gnostic individualism a threat to the centralist designs of the emerging theocracy.

Paul himself, however, was acutely aware of the need to acknowledge and maintain this vital link with the ancient Mystery wisdom. This is most evident from the manner in which he approached the wise men of Athens with his revolutionary insights.

When St. Paul, in the course of one of his great missionary endeavours, was preaching in this ancient city, his words were met with the greatest of interest, especially by the philosophically and religiously-minded people there. They took to listening to him to such an extent that he was eventually given the great opportunity to address their famous philosophical court, the Council of the Areopagus, one of the most distinguished assemblies of the old Greek world which met on the Hill of Mars.

The men of this gathering presented Paul and his

insights with a great challenge indeed, for undoubtedly they would have been thoroughly familiar with all the extant Mystery wisdom and knowledge of the day, with all the theologies, angelologies, and philosophical systems available in the world at that spiritually and culturally vibrant time and place.

The manner in which Paul met this challenge is most significant, because he felt compelled, through the power of his own particular initiation into the spiritual Presence of Christ in the world, to draw attention to the fact that now all Mystery or initiation knowledge had been totally renewed. Not only that, but even those aspects of it which were hitherto not understood, now stood fully revealed in and to the world. All of this was due to the person of Jesus Christ and his supreme act of sacrifice. Paul expounded his teaching very ingeniously by drawing his distinguished listeners' attention to the fact that the 'unknown God' of their own religions,[17] the One but secret God who stood behind all the most ancient Mystery religions of the world, is none other than Jesus Christ himself!

It was obviously *this* aspect of Paul's knowledge more than anything else which most excited, fascinated and stirred the Athenians into giving him a greater hearing than he might otherwise have received. For in it they deeply sensed that, if true, it represented something important, vital, and essentially new in the spiritual life of civilized man. The hidden and secret God of the Mysteries finally revealed, Paul was brazenly telling them! There is no more need of images of him other than the one you can learn to see with your own inner eye, the eye of your heart, of your soul, the eye in fact of purest Sophia-imbued spiritual love. The old ways of secret magical initiation, confined to a chosen or specially selected few, are truly over, he was saying. A new era in the history of man was beginning. Now each man can learn the truth about the One God and even see him for himself imaged forth in the world in the One man who stood, lived and died as a representative both of God himself and of all men for all time: the Godman Jesus Christ.

But although the Athenians were thoroughly interested in Paul's teaching they were also dumbfounded when the kernel of it, the axis upon which it revolved and without which it fell utterly apart, became fully apparent. The Athenians were indeed willing to listen, debate, speculate, and argue, but in the final analysis their capacity for faith was too weak and lacked the flesh-and-blood warmth needed to accept the core truth of St. Paul's proclamation, i.e. the astonishing reality of the Incarnation as the apotheosis of the power of love. For this indeed was its kernel! Love, however, to these learned gentlemen, represented something entirely different from what Paul had to reveal about it. And this was where the real difficulties lay. Sophisticated argument and debate was something the Athenians were no doubt very good at and loved to indulge in; but the idea of 'love incarnate' was something they had much difficulty with.

THE GOSPEL OF LOVE

Paul's teaching, however, deeply emphasized that love alone was the route now to be taken by all those who wished to acquire knowledge of God. It was a teaching that was at once both spiritually profound and humanly simple, but in this very combination lay its great power, wisdom and wide appeal. It was a way for shepherds as well as kings, as the Gospel's nativity story beautifully illustrates. The life of feeling was thus to be raised to a level on par with, if not actually higher than, the life of thought itself. It was, however, this dual nature of love which also constituted the stone on which the men of Athens stumbled, for simple, shepherd-like, loving humility was hardly a feature that figured prominently in the hearts of these serious-minded, debate-loving and sophisticated statesmen.

The writer of the Acts, however, was inspired to draw attention to this episode in Paul's life because he knew, like Paul himself, that the new Way of the spirit ushered in through Christ only made sense when knowledge of it was linked and even integrated very consciously with the Mystery wisdom and temple knowledge that existed in the world from the remotest aeons of antiquity. Because of this the learned men of Athens certainly sensed 'something' in Paul's teaching, but they lacked either the simplicity or the wisdom (or both) to be moved by the Gospel in any significant way.

Not all of them were of such a hardened disposition, however. Perhaps not in Athens, but in other places many of the 'initiates' were won over to the Gospel and they soon constituted a significant part of the early congregations of the new Church of Christ.[18] In Athens, however, we know from the Acts of the Apostles that at least one distinguished initiate was converted by Paul. And indeed it was this one vitally important individual who proved to be instrumental in maintaining for the later Church the crucial if tenuous link with the ancient Mystery wisdom which was so prominent a feature of the very early Church.

The individual to whom we refer is known as Dionysius the Areopagite (so named because he was a member of the above-mentioned Areopagus Assembly), and his significance in the history of the Church is almost of an order equal to that of Paul himself, although as yet this is not generally recognized. Nevertheless, acceptance of the relevance of Dionysius to a proper understanding of the relationship between the ancient wisdom and the new Christian Way is gradually growing, and as it does the stature of Dionysius increases accordingly. More than anyone else, even more than Paul himself in a certain sense, it is through Dionysius (who became Paul's pupil) that this link is most cogently established. And as such a link becomes more and more necessary for the Church to recognize, so too will the place of Dionysius in it gain its deserved and proper recognition.

CHAPTER SIX

THE BIRTH OF THE HERETIC AND THE 'HOUSE ARREST' OF THE SPIRIT

We shall in a later chapter deal more thoroughly with the question of Dionysius the Areopagite (see Chapter 9). For now however, it is necessary to establish a way of recognizing those forces within the body of the new Christian movement which, after Paul's initial foundational work had been done, soon began to militate against the proclamation of the pure, open, free, and essentially esoteric spirit of Paul and the other early initiates.

This repressive trend within the new movement showed itself from an early date and has, needless to say, a very complex genesis. It would be all too easy to form misguided opinions and conclusions about it, and, as so often happens with those who are misinformed regarding the deeper truth of the Christ Being, evolve personal attitudes towards the Christian movement which in reality amount to nothing less than a throwing out of the baby with the bathwater! A certain emotional tolerance which takes into account the all-too-common weakness inherent in human nature, and which it is the very business of religion and spirituality to sensibly manage, must come into play here. It is only possible to be tolerant in one's attitude to this repression, early institutionalized in the Church, if one attempts to gain a sense not only of the magnitude of the perceived implications for the whole world occasioned by the Incarnation, but also for the great practical and intellectual difficulties attendant upon its proper elucidation and evangelization. These are the very kinds of tensions which constituted, one can say, the fundamental dynamic of The Gnosis. Let us therefore look more closely at all of this.

Once word of it began to spread, the Incarnation quickly became the centre-point of a kind of spiritual vortex towards which every conceivable philosophical, theological, and mythological interpretation of the world and man became drawn, and against which all extant Mystery knowledge and wisdom soon came to be measured. A diverse mix of Individuals and groups thus began to engage themselves actively with it all over the Middle East.

In our own day we have become very used to the concept, indeed the proliferating reality, of religious cults and sects of all kinds. However, in the early Gnosis, into which the light of the Incarnation shone without question as a unifying, healing, and loving spiritual Presence, the divisive nature which *we* naturally associate with sects was hardly a factor in the spiritual thought and lives of those who were following the new Way. That said, given the very imperfect nature of human beings, and the conflicts that nearly always lie buried within even the most spiritually developed and outwardly placid of souls, it was inevitable that once the initial light of the Incarnation began to fade somewhat, and the pure spiritual balm of its healing became clouded, the inevitable differing interpretations of the nature of the Christ would have the effect of stirring up these inner psychic difficulties.

Thus, conflicts, personal arguments, antipathies, even downright hatreds soon began to show their all-too-human and ugly faces in the light of the Incarnation, from which nothing, after all, according to the Gospel, was to be hidden anyway. When psychological and psychic conflicts such as these are harnessed onto the spiritual potency of an event as profound and meaningful for man and the world as the Incarnation was, it is perhaps inevitable that our spiritual history would have had to witness a most extraordinary eventuality: the birth on the human level of beings which are, ideally speaking, purely spiritual or demonic in origin! For this is precisely what begins to happen in the early Church! Out of the spiritual cauldron which constituted The Gnosis, and into which every imaginable magical and mythical potion was being stirred, there was born a veritable monster, that most despised of all human types ever to exist – the heretic!

The birth of the heretic can be taken as that psychic event which marks the beginning of the end of what may be prosaically called the honeymoon of the Incarnation. By managing to give a human countenance to this ideal and conceptual device of the demonized human being, the new

Church arrogated unto herself a theocratic and spiritual power which was nothing less than universal. Sadly, however, it was also in the manner of this arrogation, i.e. in the methods the Church used to enforce this unilateral assertion of spiritual authority, that the initiatory and spiritually potent kernel of the Incarnation itself, i.e. the freedom to *choose* one's individual relationship to the Christ, was to be made totally illegitimate. A centralized and deified spiritual authority was emerging with an enormous and fearful power for both good *and* evil and one simply *had* to obey this . . . or else! (The word *heretic*, it should be carefully noted, actually means 'to choose'!) Freedom of the spirit was thus fast becoming a thing of the past!

FAITH V KNOWLEDGE – THE PERENNIAL DILEMMA

What all this means is that 'temporalism' at the expense of 'spiritualism'[19] was fast becoming that force by which the Church was gaining ground in the world as a new religious and unique institution. As indicated earlier, Christianity had somehow to find its own very clear identity as an organized power in the world in contradistinction to every other spiritual grouping of which there was a great proliferation at this time. Coming to the realization, however imperfectly, of the meaning of the Incarnation, and subsequently and inevitably speculating as to the manner of its proper evangelization, was something which taxed every soul who was drawn to Jesus Christ in the deepest and most inward of ways. On a basic level, this meant, of course, communion and community. On another level, however, it also meant teaching, learning and instruction. Understandably, many voices were beginning to assert themselves with varying degrees of intensity and often with very particular viewpoints within this thriving spiritual milieu.

There was, however, one overall linking characteristic in all of these various teachings and practices. They were invariably attempting to elaborate the ancient wisdom in the light of the Incarnation and to integrate this into the new vision which the Incarnation inspired. This of course was a spiritual work *par excellence*, and a work also indeed of knowledge, or of pure 'gnosis'. Gnosis in this sense was therefore seen to be something quite distinct from faith. The problem here, of course, was nothing new. It is a perennial problem regarding religion: the polarity of faith v knowledge. In the Gnostic Church, however, it was sharpened because of the presence in it of the by now well-developed Greek philosophical way of thinking. For knowledge has always far more to do with thought than with feelings. Faith or feelings, however, were not a problem in the early Church. One could say, in fact, that turning 'shepherd-like' in faith towards Christ was a relatively simple matter. Christ, after all, was just another name for God in the minds of ordinary people.

However, if the new faith was going to be a strong one, the reasons for turning to Christ had to be clear, especially given the milieu in which the new Christian community was being formed. As such, the new faith demanded great articulation on the part of those who would wish to become the leaders or elucidators of this growing trend towards belief in Christ as opposed to other deities. However, it soon came to be observed by the more serious minded and erudite of souls who were working with Christ, that whereas the Gnostic aspect of the new religion led far too easily into airy-fairy speculation about this, that, and every other blessed thing, the faith aspect was a much more practical and down-to-earth affair. Thus, faith as such had much more appeal and far greater possibilities as an instrument, a tool, or a power by or through which the newly emerging and necessary Church institutions could be forged. To these realists, faith was seen to be far more manageable in its dynamics than knowledge or gnosis. And this knowledge aspect, it was construed, would be far better left to those who could be trusted to properly dispense it, or even dispense with it, in the overall interests of the growing movement, the latter course eventually being the adopted one.

It was thus through the restrictive tendencies characteristic of less spiritually adventurous and more worldly souls who advocated such a path, that the young Christian movement was able to establish its identity by a gradual eschewing of the Mystery knowledge. Gnosis, in other words, was abandoned in favour of a far more faith-orientated constitution, a faith allied now, alas, to the predominantly temporal vision which followed as a matter of course upon the abandonment of the spirit-imbued Mystery knowledge.

Though in time the writings of St. Paul took on the status of scripture and eventually were even to become the largest single part of the official New Testament Canon, the great irony is that the Church formed itself into its deified universality and global Catholic unity by effectively side-lining the importance and meaning of their primary content!

It may be, of course, that there was no other way to forge this unity! This, however, does not alter the ambiguity inherent in the whole process. The superiority of Paul's initiatory authority shines through so strongly in his writings that they could not and cannot possibly be ignored by anyone who desires true knowledge of the Incarnation. Yet what Paul was essentially saying all through his writings could not but in a sense give rise to the very kinds of speculation that the Church wished to stamp out! For Paul was in truth endeavouring always to point out the way in which each individual could attain or aspire to the grand initiation he himself had received on the road to Damascus. The very manner and method by which he had come to know the Sophia-Christ meant that he could not but do otherwise. Thus, in many ways he was (to bluntly turn around one of his own very well-known phrases) a spiritual thorn in the side of the Church!

The unity eventually attained by the Church in this less than straightforward fashion in its dealing with the initiate Paul and his writings could therefore of course be only temporary, somewhat artificial, surely temporal, and most certainly not of a truly spiritual nature. The subsequent history and current state of the Christian movement prove this beyond dispute. The great mystery indeed of Christianity surely has as much to do with the fact that it still exists in the world as something of a coherent or clearly identifiable spiritual force after two thousand years of its confused, traumatic, and turbulent history, as it does with the miraculous nature of the Event which constitutes its spiritual core! This strength and continued relevance of Christianity to the world, in its turn, is certainly due in no small measure to the fact that the Christ Being continued and still continues to empower individuals in esoteric, inward, or even mystical, as well as, of course, in more outward, ways. And Paul's writings have very much to do with all this!

The attraction and spiritual superiority of Paul's letters lie in the fact that they highlight the essential and necessary mystical core of Christianity while yet combining this with the wide-awake clarity of pure conceptual thinking. In reading Paul's letters one cannot but be struck by the manner in which he struggles to awaken people out of an older, more symbolic type of consciousness, and into one based on a clear perception of the *word*. In this sense we can say that, for his time, Paul was being thoroughly scientific. Furthermore, Paul's writings form a perfect balance to the somewhat allegorical, often parabolic, or even symbolic, nature of the Gospel stories themselves. We need have no qualms in asserting, therefore, that any future re-integration of the mystery nature of Christ into the body of Christianity will have to take this aspect of the writings of St. Paul fully and unambiguously into account. This eventuality will, of course, constitute a great strengthening of the spiritual power of pure Christianity, for it will highlight the prophetic nature and all-embracing inclusiveness of the spirit of Sophia herself, the undoubted source of Paul's inspiration.

****

By the 4th century the strategy which the literalist Christians were using to establish an orthodoxy, i.e. the separating of faith from knowledge, produced its dividends, for by then a powerful new and fully-fledged religion had arrived on the scene! The Christians had managed to establish themselves in the world by rooting out what now came to be regarded with ever increasing venom as the 'Gnostic heresies'. The Church was now busy with the serious work of evolving what amounted to an increasingly hate-filled theology of heresy.

This was something which revealed the full extent of its latent and awful demonic power with the inception of that most fearsome and vile of all male-dominated institutions ever conceived by human kind – the Holy Inquisition of the Middle Ages.

In splitting off reason, knowledge, and wisdom as an ideal to be cultivated by all and not just by a privileged priesthood (and this essentially is what the rejection of The Gnosis amounted to!), the suppressed light of the benign spirit of Sophia could hardly work openly in the world any more. What was even worse, however, is that this spirit was manipulated, twisted, and turned into its very opposite, the spectral or death-like shadow of a darkened spiritual power which finds its spiritual food deep in the baser instincts of the human psyche.

This is the self-same negative power which in a spiritual sense has man's proneness to sin as its template and, even worse, has the very embodiment of evil as its goal. It is, moreover, a subtle, archetypal, and highly persuasive power, deceptive in the extreme, which lends itself very easily to those who, for whatever reason, are prepared to exploit it for their own dubious ends. Such exploitation, ultimately of course serving the purposes of evil, is always evident anywhere goodness and wisdom are abandoned.

THE WESTERN CONSCIOUSNESS IS SPLIT

It was in this way that the consciousness of Western man was painfully split and exploited spiritually. The Inquisition may be regarded as nothing less than an inevitable, albeit blasphemous, outcome of a hate-filled trend within the Church, a trend which began once the pure spiritual light of the Holy Sophia was denied access to the dark and often blood-letting faiths of primitive or tribal man. It must be remembered that this type of faith constituted, by and large, the chief demographic characteristic of the place where Christianity was gaining its firmest footing in the world, i.e. continental Europe. This category of individual, i.e. the tribal man, thus supplied not only the obedient spirits that every faith needs to give it some kind of legitimate power, but it also supplied the necessary 'cannon-fodder' for the increasingly aggressive *realpolitik* that the Church was ever more tightly embracing.

Needless to say, none of this should be allowed to detract from the great amount of good that Christians have achieved down the ages. It is very significant, however, that this good is often traceable to single or outstanding *individuals* whose understanding of the Christ Being could go beyond the limits fixed by the doctrinal norms or orthodoxy, and penetrate into a direct knowledge of the spiritual world and its angelic inhabitants. The case of St. Francis is perhaps one of the best-known examples of those few individuals who somehow always managed to slip through the orthodox net of their time, however rigid or fine-meshed it may have been, and in so doing could bring the light of the pure spirit to bear upon the often materialistically clouded vision of their contemporaries.

It is obvious, however, from any spiritually informed appraisal of the history of organized Christianity that the divine light which powered into the world through the advent of the Incarnation was never meant to be either fugitive in its appearance or in any way restricted or selective in its application. The forces of temporalism and materialism, however, powerful as they always are in influencing man's all-too-human nature, early opposed the entry into this nature of the divine spiritual element, this miraculous phenomenon uniquely enacted by and poured into the world through the Incarnation.

The mortal body of flesh and blood, transformed by Christ's Deed into a shining, living temple of God, an ethereal body freely given, through Christ's supreme sacrifice, as a gift to the world in which every man could have a share through his being membered into it through the Kyrios[22] – this began, after the initial flood of the glorious light of the Resurrection had receded, to give way to the outmoded forces of death and decay once more. Mere tablets of Law began to replace those pure draughts of angelic enlightenment which gave to the very first Christians the power to discern in the Incarnation the *fact* of spiritual resurrection or rebirth, and the Church soon had far more to do with cold stones, chapels and their attendance, privileged priests and so on, than it had with the living and immanent Presence of the spirit of the ethereal Sophia-Christ.

PAGAN SUN WORSHIP

Despite the fact that the troublesome Gnostics had been more or less annihilated by the end of the 3rd century, the early Church nevertheless could not avoid remaining tinged, to some degree at least, with what from then on would be disparagingly labelled as paganism.[20] However, it was this colouring, this delicate tint of the ancient Mystery wisdom that lingered on within the Church which made it attractive to followers of the many pagan cults operating in the Roman Empire at this time, cults whose potential for satisfying ambitions, spiritual or otherwise, was fast diminishing compared to the exciting, new, and modern Christians.

Let us look, therefore, at the psycho/spiritual dynamics behind all this, for they are truly intriguing.

Pagan Sun worship had been undoubtedly thrown into great confusion once the more sensitive, spiritually minded, and influential souls who adhered to it began to realize what the Incarnation really meant. They had slowly come to realize that this Sun which they saw moving in the sky, rising in the east or setting in the west, could no longer be regarded as merely some object out there which they could only know or worship in an indirect, abstract or some other symbolic way. Something extraordinary and incredible, something almost indeed beyond belief, was now beginning to enter their consciousness and their spiritual life. Now in very truth the spiritual Being of this Sun was felt to have entered into the dying temporal word, and by virtue of this miraculous fact they could, through an initiation experience, actually feel that it was somehow not outside them anymore, but was now to be found rising inside their very own spiritually enlivened bodies!

The combined focus of the entire ancient wisdom had pointed to the fact that the Sun God, the Solar Logos, was drawing nearer and nearer to the Earth as the aeons passed, and then most wondrously, had actually incarnated in the flesh. The God, the divinity, was now conceived to have not only entered into the Earth itself, but also into the very body and soul of man. This was the Incarnation. It was an Event, a revelation with the most shattering and far-reaching of consequences imaginable for the individual who approached it.

It was also, however, a revelation which, once fully absorbed, begged the huge question as to the proper method and manner of its dissemination in the world. It was therefore a time of great soul-searching, a time for the deepest thinking, and of course a time especially for the most careful of utterances and written word-formulas.

With this sublime knowledge lying at the very heart of Christianity, however encrusted over it may have gradually become by dogma and theology, the Christians could not but eventually have become a powerful religious force in the world over and above the claims of their pagan contemporaries. For the Incarnation had effected something in the world which was not merely cultic, mythic, psychic, or even occult in its implications. It was indeed all of these. But through it the very substance of the Earth itself was deemed to have been changed, to have been altered for the good. It was felt that into the very composting matter of the planet Earth, a divine injection had been made. Through Christ's sacrifice a mysterious

Sun-like substance was, in short, conceived to have fallen to the Earth and entered into the very bloodstream of mankind! And by virtue of this 'homeopathic' miracle, a new evolutionary impulse was seen to have entered the world, giving to human and merely earth-born faculties a powerful new visionary and even divine possibility.

It can be seen from all of this that the forces at work in the making of our human history are often of the very essence of what is most fascinating and indeed almost imponderable! Even with the light of the little understanding of it that circulated in Palestine in the centuries immediately after the Incarnation, we should not be surprised at the fact that Christianity, after being initially subjected to much suspicion, repression, and persecution, was eventually legitimized.

CONSTANTINE THE GREAT

It was the Emperor Constantine the Great (born c. 274) who was the one responsible for this move towards legitimacy for the Christians. But there was at the same time a certain amount of inevitability attached to Constantine's action, for he was deeply aware of the soul and spirit power of the ancient Mysteries, especially those connected with the Sun. There is indeed evidence to suggest that he was an initiate of one of the pagan Sun cults of the time.[21] As Emperor he was of course also a man of the world *par excellence*.

Thus, temporal as well as spiritual matters always weighed heavily upon his mind, and no doubt he thought deeply as to how he could put his spiritual knowledge into the service of his purely temporal needs and designs. In this way, his Sun initiation was to become a powerful and highly useful weapon for regulating and ordering the turbulent and often subconscious impulses at work within his all-too-human realm. And the Christians, he gradually became aware, held the trump card in this respect! Furthermore, by Constantine's time the new Church was perceived as being a force that simply *had* to be reckoned with in the world, one way or the other, so better use it to the best advantage!

While hardly a Christian, it is true that Constantine was able to relate to the Christ Being in a certain way. But the manner in which this relationship was expressed is very revealing about how far the fabulous vision, which was so alive and so actively cultivated by the very early Christians, had fallen away from its original grandeur and pristine purity. This tremendous vision was one which represented to the followers of the new Way that the body of the new Church was identical with the body of the risen Christ.[22] Certainly by Constantine's time this primary initiatory vision had faded, and had even undergone a process of decay from its original incarnational view of the human body of flesh and blood as a living temple of the Christ Being himself.

This wonderful pristine vision of the Kyrios or Church had gradually turned into one far more concerned with cold stone than with living flesh. It was in a sense a looking backwards to the old pillars of a religion based on dead letters chiselled onto stone tablets, something which had been totally fulfilled, superseded, and rendered outmoded by the Event of the Incarnation. Stones (no matter how beautiful a form they may have been given by skilled artisans or artists) could never again, from the first Easter Sunday morning when the stone was rolled away from the empty tomb, be anything other than backward-looking or empty symbols for the new ethereal spiritual reality released into the world through the Incarnation.

This was, however, a reality which was feared and shunned for many reasons by the emerging types within the new Church; suspect reasons all, not the least of which would seem to be that the Incarnation was reckoned to be far too good to be true in the first place!

At the very least, it was a truth which could only be profitably dealt with by turning it into a mere object of faith. In the process, however, it became banished into the dark depths of the unconscious mind and there left to accrue its doubtful interest. To aspire to a clear-headed, purposeful, and practical knowledge of the Incarnation seemed to mean nothing less than risking one's sanity within a maze of competing angelologies, intellectual wrangling and hair-splitting definitions, into which no amount of mere words was deemed capable of bringing order.

Faith, dogma, law and order; it was these, therefore, and the mentality which they bred, that now, by the 4th century, had become the chief determinants of the Church's emerging constitution. The spirit behind the letter and the law, that subtle discerning ability which had been the quintessential characteristic of the very early Christians and which had promised, and often delivered, initiatory understanding and knowledge of Christ to all who came under its influence, this was now rapidly drying up in the heat of the theological warfare which came to a head in Constantine's time.

The issues in this warfare were subtle, complex, and often highly charged emotionally. Given the dogmatic nature of the disputes generally, the principal one was, needless to say, centred upon the correct definition of God himself. Quite understandably, from *its* viewpoint, the growing Roman style of orthodoxy wished to establish the fact that Jesus Christ was God once and for all, Trinity or no Trinity! In doing this they wished to silence what they considered to be all the divisive chatter about it!

THE CASE OF GENTLE ARIUS

Gnosticism had been quite left behind by this stage. But these kinds of troubles were far from over for the emerging orthodoxy, and one of the biggest threats to this orthodoxy was the way of approaching the mystery of the Incarnation which became associated with the theologian Arius. This style of exegesis thus acquired the name of Arianism. Essentially, what Arius was saying was that you can't dogmatically assert, as the orthodox theologians were doing, that there are three persons in the One God and then turn this into a hell-binding article of faith, expecting ordinary people to believe in something which was, quite simply, incomprehensible. For it *was* in point of fact incomprehensible, even to philosophers and theologians themselves! Thus, while never denying Christ's divinity, Arius maintained that Christ himself must be distinguished or distinguishable from God the Father. However, his manner of apprehending and teaching this distinction undoubtedly leaned far too heavily, for orthodoxy's liking, towards a Gnostic approach to the Trinity. Arius could never hammer his knowledge or image of God into the straitjacketed or sterile Trinity of this emerging orthodoxy. He and his followers were thus not tolerated by the hard-heads, though Arius himself tried heroically to please them.

And so the sweet-tempered and saintly Arius, this father of the emerging orthodoxy's most hated so-called heresy, was by some accounts poisoned just before he was prepared to make a grand gesture of reconciliation in Constantinople in 336. We may say that such an eventuality for him, if true, fits the emerging picture of, and practises within, the new Church very well! For in truth Arianism *had* to be got rid of completely, once and for all, smelling as it did of the increasingly despised Gnosticism, the last traces of which the dogmatic Church was now violently in the process of eliminating.

Though this elimination of Arius was drastic, he, his knowledge and his teaching nevertheless had a huge following, and Arianism lingered on as a threat to the Roman Church's authority for many centuries afterwards.

JESUS, THE ANGRY MAN!

We have hitherto been indicating the manner in which the new Church was gradually turning away from the early and truly spiritual vision of its mission and purpose in the world. The original inspiration was that via the Incarnation, the old temple wisdom was seen to have taken on a completely new form. Thus, in a totally real sense, the temple and its wisdom had actually *become man* through the spiritual power of the Incarnation. This was the very essence of the first Christians' understanding of the meaning of their

Church. The word 'church' itself indicates this very well, coming as it does from the Greek word Kyrios, meaning 'Lord'. This wisdom-knowledge, and the vision it engendered, began to be actively suppressed from very early on, for various reasons.

The fact that this crucial, central, and pure understanding of the Incarnation would be denied to most men and women soon after the completion of the Incarnation Event was prophetically foreseen by Christ himself. This fact is clearly indicated in the Gospel in different ways where the Pharisees and especially the Sadducees stand for the forces opposing Christ's esoteric mission, forces later embodied in Rome. It was this prophetic foreknowledge which gave rise to one of Christ' most significant actions in the whole of the Gospel.

For it quite simply made him angry!

There is no greater wrath than a divine one (as even a cursory glance at the history of Europe or of our Western civilization generally will show). It can be argued that even Christ himself said (in the Gospel of Matthew, 10:34) that he came not to bring peace, but a sword! Be that as it may, when anger and violence are used for the wrong reasons, they undoubtedly corrupt far more than they cure. For it is how and why anger is used that is the crucial factor. Used in ignorance, anger is one of the most destructive and infectious of all human emotions.

We do not normally, of course, associate anger or violence with the person or temperament of Jesus Christ. The overriding tone of the whole of the Gospel is one of a yielding forgiveness, a simplicity of faith and virtue, a message of meekness, even of passivity and pacifism. Anger has virtually no place in it at all.

There is one scene, however, in the Gospels which is totally at variance with this general tone, and it is perhaps the only instance in the whole of the Incarnation drama in which Jesus actually displays anger.[23]. Significantly, this is entirely bound up with the Temple. When he enters the Temple in Jerusalem just after he began his three-year ministry, he is angered to the point of violence by what he sees taking place there, supposedly in the name of God. Then, astonishingly, he makes a 'whip of cords' and proceeds to drive out the money-changers and the dealers in sacrificial birds who were congregated and trading there, as was their custom and practice. And with his whip he scatters them and their money in all directions in a scene of unparalleled wrath.

What a scene it is! Immediately afterwards, of course, he is severely questioned about his behaviour. By what authority does he do such astounding things? And how can he give a sign to explain such unbelievable behaviour? For in truth, given the way the Temple was regarded in the Jewish faith, his action here could be construed as nothing other than supreme and total blasphemy. His answers to his critics and questioners were twofold: The Temple, he said, is supposed to be the house of God, but you have made of it a den of thieves! And as for signs, he said: 'Pull this Temple down and I will rebuild it in three days.'[24]

Undoubtedly through this important incident, occurring at the very beginning of his three-year ministry (in John's account), Jesus is alluding to something archetypal. And it is this: In the most pointed and dramatic of all possible terms, the deepest and truest nature of the Christ's Being and his mission on Earth are being emphasised. The Gospel is here very graphically illustrating the fact that a true divining of the nature of Christ Jesus reveals him to have entered the world primarily in order to destroy the old way of life, the outdated modes of culture, the dried-up practices in religion and initiation, all of which of course placed the temple at the very centre! This old, hard, and secret way of the stone temple, he was saying in the most emphatic terms, was now outlived, outworn, and only capable, if perpetuated, of breeding confusion, division, and corruption. In referring to the destruction of the Temple and its rebuilding in three days, he was indicating allegorically the way in which his mission on Earth was to be miraculously fulfilled. For he was soon, he knew, to die physically, only to arise again from the tomb three days afterwards in a new, etheric or spiritual body, the beauty and magnificence of which Paul and many others were soon after the event to behold.

We would be claiming no high ground at all, therefore, if, given the subsequent development of his Church, we were to cultivate a mood of moral empathy with this action of Christ as he drives away the money lenders from the Temple! Though he completed his appointed mission and fulfilled all the highest prophesies appertaining to him and the divine plan for man and the world, nevertheless the Church he came to inaugurate, i.e. the temple of stone turned into one of spirit flesh-and-blood, quickly got overtaken by the 'money-changers' again. Worldly forces, in other words, more to do with temporal expediency than with true spiritual enlightenment, soon began to gain momentum within the body of the emerging and physically strengthening Church. Thus, in driving away the money-men he was expressing nothing less than a prophetic wrath, a divine anger directed not only against those present in the Temple at that particular time, but also symbolically against those forces which he knew only too well would soon raise their ugly heads again and build stone temples in his name, (and moreover use them for selling far more suspect merchandise than these bird dealers in Jerusalem ever did!).

He *knew* this would happen once his own physical presence on the Earth was there no longer. And he knew also that this temple-building was something which would be fundamentally in opposition to his Gospel.

AND THE TEMPLE BECOMES MAN

For the deepest truth of his Gospel lay in the fact that the old temple was never to be raised up again, except in the flesh. No matter how magnificent a church or a cathedral may have been, the fact was that by cultivating such a church or temple-building trend, God would be once more locked up inside temples of stone.[25]

It made Christ angry to perceive this eventuality. What he could foresee was that the inner voice of the pure, bright, and free spirit, which was meant, through the power of his incarnational Gospel, to infuse and transform the very flesh and blood of Everyman via his being membered into the living body of the new Church, was in danger of being replaced by the strong, stone-hard, and often dark power of the pulpit, something indeed which eventually came about. The 'reason' for this was that the spirit itself was eventually deemed to be far too dangerous a thing for the ordinary man in the street to know or possess, and it therefore had in effect to be put under 'house arrest'!

The truth of all this is well borne out by what started to happen in the Church as soon as it became officially sanctioned within the Empire, something which happened during Emperor Constantine's rule.

Once the Sophia spirit which permeated the very early Christian movement had finally been put away and the Church was about to take a big worldly leap forward, what do we find? Stone church-building on a grand scale! Emboldened if not truly inspired by Christ, Constantine soon set about a church-building programme which by the time he died apparently amounted to no less than 21. Though one of these, the church of St. George in Constantinople, soon afterwards became (and still is) the site of one of the most beautiful churches in Christendom and was renamed (significantly) the Church of Sophia, nevertheless the trend was well and truly set. The living God was being locked up once more inside temples of stone!

Thus, the legitimizing of Christianity in the Roman Empire clearly marks the end of the first phase of Christianity's development. The light of The Gnosis having been well and truly quenched, the Church now embarked on a phase of development which is largely temporal. In tandem with this, the wisdom-eschewing, albeit faith-espousing orthodoxy is becoming fully established. However, even from the time of Constantine, hair-splitting debates were taking place in the Church that eventually caused a major crack to appear even within this orthodoxy itself. It is fairly obvious when studying these debates that no real solution, in fact no real understanding of them is possible while the banished Sophia wisdom is not available to shed its light. It was also because of this that these ostensibly religious debates often appear to descend into little more than mere political manoeuvring. It is from this manoeuvring only that their apparent absurdity may be somewhat excused.

THE GREAT SCHISM

Given the turmoil that was now generally brewing throughout the whole of the Empire, political manoeuvring was becoming a veritable art, and one moreover which involved very high political stakes; indeed, the stakes could hardly have been higher, for they were nothing less than the very unity of the Empire itself! Though the final official split in the Church between East and West (the Great Schism) did not formally take place until 1054, such an eventuality was actually a long time looming.

The machinations and horse-trading which led to this split in the Church are, needless to say, subtle and complex in the extreme, but one pertinent observation must be made here regarding it. That is that the schism represented the total cutting off of the Western Church from perhaps its deepest source of inspiration, a separation the consequences of which the Eastern Church itself was only too well aware of. For, as we shall presently show, it was from the Eastern portion of the Church's temporal body, right up to the 9th century, that pressure was being exerted which endeavoured to keep a line of contact open with the very early Church and the ancient wisdom, however tenuous and progressively weaker this link may have become as the centuries with their wrangling progressed. But the Roman Catholic orthodoxy would have none of it! In Chapter 10 we shall see much more clearly what actually happened here, but the final result was the triumph of the Roman militant orthodoxy in the West and the eventual decline of its culture into the unabashed materialism it now extols, while in the East, in the Church and in its culture generally, at least a flavour of the true spirit of Sophia was, and still is, alive.

CHAPTER SEVEN

THE HOLY LAND OF ERIN COMES TO THE RESCUE

In the introduction to this book, we called attention to the fact that Christianity had from the very outset two distinct 'flavours', an Eastern and a Western one. These differences in the manner of apprehending the Incarnation and the cultic and civilizing influences which flowed from it obviously became more pronounced as the centuries passed, but a clear recognition that they were there from the very beginning, as well as some understanding of the nuances which constituted these differences, will inevitably help towards an appreciation of just what or who Sophia was perceived to be in these ancient times.

That there are very distinct differences in the spirituality generally, Christian or otherwise, of East and West is probably too obvious an observation to elaborate on here.

This is very apparent to anyone who has any interest in, or knowledge of, the subject of spirituality. This difference comes perhaps to its most obvious manifestation in what may be regarded as the robust or masculine 'practicality' of the Western approach, as opposed to the more effeminate or 'ethereality' of the Eastern way. These two, fundamentally opposing cultural tendencies, undoubtedly profoundly influenced the development and eventual split of the Church into Eastern and Western blocs.

In the very far west, however, that is in Ireland, the manner in which Christianity took root reveals something of its truly universal nature. It was there, it seems, that there came about a happy blend of these two erstwhile opposing facets, so that the mystery or ethereal side of the Incarnation did not come into such conflict with the more historical or down-to-earth aspects as it obviously did in other places. In other words, in this weird and wonderful land of Erin, a cultural as well as a religious unity could be maintained with regard to the Gospel and its dissemination, which would in time become the very model of a true and practical, yet fully spiritual, Christianity. In Ireland, the Gospel had found perhaps the most fertile soil in the world in which to grow in its esoteric or most inward manner. Long after this inwardness or freedom of its spirit had been more or less spent or banished, both in the field of its genesis (the East generally) as well as in its later development on continental Europe, it remained green and alive in Ireland.

Thus it was that here it came to its full flowering in the 5th - 8th centuries, a period which is known to earlier historians of Ireland as that of the Celtic Church, but may perhaps more accurately be described nowadays as the

Gaelic Church. This was a short but Golden Age of Christianity which is becoming increasingly recognized as having been nothing less than the source of that light which kept the lamp of civilization aglow in an increasingly darkened world.

THE CELTIC CHURCH

This phenomenon of the Gaelic or Celtic Church and its background we will now look at closely, for in doing so we will be able all the more readily to gain a practical understanding of the inherent spiritual/religious power of the Incarnation itself, as well as some working knowledge as to the manner in which this spiritual power was effectively depotentized or destroyed. In other words, we will learn to understand how what should have been a primary factor in the later development of mainstream, exoteric, and especially Western culture was banished underground to become esoteric instead.

Even long before Christianity was ever heard of anywhere in the world, the ancient land of Hibernia (the Romans' name for Ireland) was held in the highest esteem by wise men, for it was considered by them as a dwelling place fit even for the gods themselves! All ancient lands inevitably have their own particular air of mystery. It has always been recognized, however, that Ireland lays claim to a special magic all of its own. Even a little knowledge of the modern country can convince one fairly easily as to why this should be the case. There just seems to be something in the very air, especially as one goes farther south on the island! The elements combine and work together here in the atmosphere of Ireland to create a landscape of such soft and virginal beauty that one may yet, especially on fine days in spring or early summer, get a sense of how and why the ancients regarded this place as a piece of Paradise.

The Sun divinity, too, the Solar Logos, had an ancient mystic and mythical attachment to Ireland. Long before this spirit ever came into an historical association with the Earth through the Incarnation, the very oldest books in the world, those written in Sanskrit, had referred to Ireland as 'Hiranya', which means the 'Island of the Sun'. Furthermore, Ireland was also known as the very 'Garden of Phoebus'. (Phoebus is one of the oldest names in the world for the god of the Sun, Apollo.) Even the Gaelic word for Sun, 'graine', was, according to the first century B.C. writer and esotericist, Virgil, another name for Apollo!

Given the perennial nature of the cloudy and often misty weather in Ireland, it may seem a bit strange at first why this place should be the home of such a pure and cultic Sun-worship for it to be regarded as the very home of Apollo. This, however, is nothing to be puzzled about once we begin to realize something of the depth, profundity, and spiritual sophistication of the culture and civilization which existed in Ireland in prehistoric times. At the head of this culture, nurturing, guiding, and instructing it in every aspect of its needs and development, were a special class of people whose wisdom, knowledge, and craft ranked equally as high, if not indeed higher, than the priest-king initiates of the ancient Egyptian civilization at the height of *its* achievements. These were none other than the famous Druids, a clear image of whom we need to have if we are to properly evaluate the Sun-inspired nature of the ancient culture of Hibernia. These were people whose highly trained spiritual and magical powers easily penetrated the atmospheric vapours of the merely physical world and its clouds, an art empowering them ultimately to behold the majesty of the Sun-Being in all his spiritual beauty, glory, and divine power.

THE QUESTION OF ATLANTIS

We are talking here of a time prior to the arrival of the Celts in Ireland, of a civilization that stretches so far back into the mists of time that some say (and the great Greek philosopher Plato was one of these!) that it can only be truly accounted for by seeking its origin in a totally lost civilization which had its geographical location centred somewhere out in what is now the Atlantic Ocean. We speak of course of the legendary Atlantis, the possible existence of which can still excite the imaginatively inquiring mind quite as much now as it did in Plato's time, for the simple reason that the time scales involved are so great that the only true measuring instrument for them can be none other than the imaginative power of the soul herself!

The ancient wisdom tells how this continent of Atlantis, as well as virtually its entire culture and civilization, was submerged in the rising waters of the ocean. Esoteric literature sometimes states that the reason for this catastrophe was that the Atlantean initiates became, over time, decadent and eventually abused and misused their very great magical powers. In doing this, they also triggered atmospheric and climatic changes which caused (obviously over very long periods of time) the Earth's oceans to rise. Eventually this led to the alteration of the entire physiognomy of the Globe itself.

Whatever one's attitude to this theory may be, however, it must be accepted that what is generally referred to as The Flood or The Deluge is an indisputable event in the prehistory of the world, traces of which can be found in the mythology of peoples virtually everywhere. In the more specific terms of the history of Western spirituality, this event is recorded in the Bible as marking the beginning of a new epoch in man's relationship (covenant) with God.

Regarding Atlantis, however, it was Solon the Wise (6th century B.C.) who told Plato that the Egyptian Initiates had told him that it had disappeared 9000 years before their own (the Egyptians) time! This partly is the reason why Ireland would have been held in such high esteem by the ancients of the East. For them, Ireland was a tiny remnant of that fabulous though almost forgotten land in the far, far west, a land full of mystery and magic which had been all but submerged in the Deluge. This would also certainly explain why Hibernia was known to the ancients as the Garden of Phoebus, a last little bit of a lost paradisal civilization remaining on the Earth, a wondrous place certainly, and one where the almost forgotten gods of the Atlanteans still lived and were known to its people.

THE HIBERNIAN MYSTERIES

Indeed, when one considers the very special case of the Hibernian Mysteries[26] one can hardly doubt but that in the minds of the ancients Ireland represented a vital link with a virtually unknown or forgotten pre-history of the Earth, of its civilizations and its gods. Knowledge of the Hibernian Mysteries reveals that they had the possibility to evoke or create a synthesis of the combined wisdom of *all* of the other extant Mysteries. The ancients would have been acutely aware of this and it would undoubtedly have deeply influenced their attitude to Hibernia, its people, and its wise initiates. Within the sanctums of these Hibernian Mysteries there seemed, to the ancients, to be contained the possibility for mankind of a great refinement of cultural, religious, and social life, indeed even man's very consciousness itself. The Hibernian Mysteries in other words seemed to constitute a great advance not only on what the other Mysteries actually taught, but also on what they could ever hope to achieve in the future.

As we have mentioned earlier, the Mystery religions in different parts of the world had always, from the most ancient times, venerated the divine as it came to expression in Nature around them and in the Cosmos above them. This the different races and nations cultivated in various ways, and in the process and over great expanses of time, evolved their own rituals, religious practices, initiations, and so on, all of which were based on their own particular images or understanding of the gods. However, cultivation of knowledge of the universe and the gods was such a vast enterprise that it was surely also understood by the initiates generally that no *one* particular type of initiation could ever be expected to cover every aspect of it.

In the Hibernian Mysteries, however, this challenge was taken up. For here there was available an initiation into the greatest and most profound secrets of the universe, secrets pertaining not only to the divine ordering of the world and man, but also secrets revealing the divine plan for mankind's future, a future so profound and grand that even angels could not tell of it.[27] And yet these secrets were revealed to the Hibernian Initiates!

Though there were Sun cults and Sun religions all over the ancient world, it was in Ireland that the Sun divinity revealed to the druid initiate the most universal, profound, and at the same time purely Earthly aspect of his relationship to man. This was intimately connected to the coming event which was to change the entire course of our world's history: the Incarnation. Long before this event actually took place on the Earth itself, the Initiates of the Hibernian Mysteries had been aware of its approach and had prepared for it through the rites of their initiation practices in a manner which was simply not possible for others. As a result, the whole culture of the island of Ireland was ready to receive the news of the Incarnation in a totally pure and profoundly spiritual way. To these people the Incarnation was not some strange or unlikely event to be debated and philosophized about. Quite the contrary! It was an event that was actually expected. And when it did eventually happen, it was something to be wholeheartedly participated in:

When in Palestine those remarkable occurrences took place which we describe when speaking of Christ Jesus on Golgotha and of his environment – at that very time solemn Festivals were celebrated within the Hibernian Mysteries themselves and the community associated with them, that is to say by the people who belonged in some way to the Mysteries. The events that took place in Palestine at the beginning of our era and were visible there to the physical eyes, were beheld spiritually in Hibernia. There men experienced the Mystery of Golgotha in the spirit. And this was the basis of the greatness inherent in everything that subsequently went out from Hibernia into the rest of the civilized world but disappeared as time went on.[28]

That Christianity took hold in Ireland in a somewhat mysterious way is actually well known to scholars. It is a mystery, however, which will only be really solved via the foregoing insight. In Ireland, the whole phenomenon of Christianity was a totally 'organic' process.

The real facts about the Christianization of the Irish are very far removed from the 'churched' version! It is really only a sort of (Roman!) Church-inspired 'myth' to assume that it was St. Patrick who brought Christianity to Ireland. In recent years, however, this 'myth' about Ireland (and many others too, hopefully!) is gradually being dissolved.

It is quite well established by now that Christianity was cultivated here before Patrick came in 432. This is not to say, of course, that Patrick did not do powerful missionary work in Ireland. But he did not 'convert' Ireland.[29]

Indeed, if we wish to look at this phenomenon from another angle there is an old story, still very much alive in the folk memory of the Irish, which throws some very revealing light on how the Gospel came to them, and it would be worthwhile here to recount it. Apart from anything else it illustrates very well the way in which stories and legends generally, if backed up by proper insights, can give accurate and historical information about hitherto little known facts.

THE STORY OF KING CONOR AND THE DRUID
The story goes as follows:

King Conor MacNessa was the King of the northern province of Ulster. One day a battle took place in which his ally, the King of the southern province of Leinster, lost his life. However, the king's brains were taken from his head by a warrior, and a very precious sling-stone was made out of them. This treasure was then placed in King Conor's headquarters at Emain Maccha. However one day a champion of the western province of Connaught, whose name was Ket, stole it. Now eventually at a place called Ardnurchar (The Fort of the Sling-Cast) a battle was fought between the Connaught-men and the Ultonian (Ulster) warriors. King Conor was there too and when he saw the great array of beautiful Connaught ladies present he rose to the occasion and proceeded to exhibit his ferocious skills much to the jealous disapproval of the Connaught-man Ket. Ket, at a loss what to do, eventually took out his precious stolen brain-ball, put it in his sling and aimed straight at Conor. King Conor was struck between the eyes and the ball lodged firmly in his forehead. When the Ulster warriors eventually go back home with their wounded King, the Druid physician declared: 'If I take out that ball King Conor will die!' And so it was agreed to leave the ball in Conor's head. King Conor then had his forehead sewn up with golden thread and was ordered not to do anything excitable or passionate anymore.

However, one Friday afternoon, seven years later, King Conor was out riding when suddenly he saw the Sun grow mysteriously dark. He summoned one of his Druids immediately and asked him what was the meaning of this. The Druid, in a magic trance, soon proceeded to tell King Conor of a hill in Palestine on which he saw three crosses. To one of these crosses was nailed, he said, a figure like one of the Immortals. King Conor was astonished!

'Has he done wrong?' he enquired.

'No,' the Druid answered. 'This is the Son of the living God.'

The Druid then went on to tell King Conor the whole story of the Passion and death of Christ.

Conor lost his temper when he heard of this terrible outrage! He suddenly whipped his sword from its scabbard and ran wildly into a sacred grove of oak trees hacking in every direction.

'This is what I would do to his accusers,' he cried. However, in his great anger the brain-ball burst from his head and he dropped dead.[30]

What is indicated in this story is that the Druids, from within the sacred sanctums of their Mystery groves and temples in Ireland, were able to behold with their clairvoyant faculties what was actually happening in Palestine! And the 'brain ball' alluded to here clearly indicates one of the most widely known aspects of esoteric knowledge, the subtle body's inner or 'third eye', the primary organ of clairvoyant vision which is known to be located approximately in the area of the physical body's forehead.[31]

The initiates of the Mysteries could undoubtedly communicate with one another through their extrasensory powers in much the same way as modern clairvoyants can transcend physical boundaries (though it has to be said that we must be careful of making too close a comparison here). It is therefore not in the least unreasonable to assume that the Hibernian Druids' ability to 'watch' the Incarnation drama as it unfolded in Palestine would have been known to the initiates of the Eastern or other Mystery rites. And these (Eastern) initiates, who had a geographically closer contact with the events in Palestine, would have been eager to make physical contact with the spiritual Irish in order to boost their own overall knowledge and understanding of the Gospel.

Thus it is not in the least surprising that we find from the very beginning of Christianity evidence of contact between the Eastern Church and the Irish. There is a growing body of external knowledge regarding this. The desert monks of Egypt and Palestine seem the most likely and fruitful conduit of communication. The Egyptian Tau crosses of Ireland (one of which is now in the National Museum) are perhaps the most solid and enduring testaments to this early traffic between Hibernia and the Eastern Church. It would be missing the point to regard this Egyptian influence as evidence relating to the mystery of how the early evangelization of Ireland actually took place. It would be much more in keeping with the reality of the situation to assume the reverse, i.e. that *they* came to Ireland to develop and expand their own spiritual and initiatory awareness of the Christian Mystery.

For, given the parched deserts of the land from which they came, with its tradition of hard and ascetic contemplation, these monks would surely have found the soft and misty land of Erin, where the Sophia-Christ was regarded with such loving warmth, a very special place. Indeed, driven by a holy hunger and thirst for Christ as they were, an enthusiasm which regularly spilled over into the fanatical, the natural and virginal beauty of the Irish landscape must have seemed to them little short of Paradise itself.

SUN AND CROSS

There was no threat here, they must have instinctively felt, of the new, wonderfully free God of love being locked up inside stuffy old pyramids of stone, in secret temples, or even modern churches! No! They would have been moved to the very quick of their being by the freedom of the Holy Sophia Spirit and how here she wrought Christ from out of the very soil itself and into the new and consciously Christian soul of Ireland.

In Hibernia it was Nature herself, in all her grandeur, grace, and ineffable beauty, which was the temple. This is not to say the 'hard stuff', the 'spirit of stone' as it were, would have no place in the Irish consciousness as it learned and developed its new relationship with Christ. Quite the contrary! For here stone was to become the matter of a profound artistic/religious impulse stemming directly from the Incarnation, but one which nevertheless would express the free spirit of the Celtic soul. Here, therefore, stone was not to be the cause of shutting up the spirit of God inside church and temple buildings, but rather the occasion for chiselling its hardness into a musicality of expression unsurpassable in its spiritual dignity. We refer here to the famous and beautiful decorated high stone crosses of the Irish Celtic church. In this ancient Irish art of the high stone Sun-crosses of Christ we have evidence of a stone-craft, monolithic in its depth and span of knowledge, which, when combined with the incarnational impulse, was brought to a lofty and spiritual perfection.

Furthermore, these old Irish Celtic crosses are excellent examples of an art which mark, and through which we may wondrously observe, the unique transition from one epoch – the descending and earthbound history of man, ancient and cosmic beyond all imagining – to a new, light-filled era of free ascension; an ever higher form of consciousness imparted through Christ, making us co-creators with God of a new heaven and a new earth, as stated in the Gospel.

On these crosses the decorative images are always scenes taken from the Gospel story, as well as from the Old Testament. But the formal motif, the cross or crossbars projecting outwards from the central Sun-disc, was a form and an image used in the cultic life of the people of this land for millennia before these crosses were made. (Wonderful examples of these cosmic Sun-cross discs, finely wrought in pure gold and said to date back to 2,500 B.C., can be seen in the National Museum in Dublin.)

Christ himself is invariably placed at the centre of the cosmic Sun-disc of the stone crosses. Often his arms and hands are outstretched, indicating the manner, as much as the inevitability, of his death in or upon the physical planet of the Earth itself, which the bars of the cross represent. All of this directs our attention to the divine Solar Logos as the One destined from the beginning to descend from the cosmic Sun heights and incarnate, even unto death, as one of *us* here on Earth.

THE TUATHA DE DANANN

The prehistory of Ireland, and indeed its 'real' history, is full of accounts of descendings, invasions, and conquests. In fact, one of the best-known sources of Irish mythological stories is called The Book of Invasions! Perhaps the most famous of these mythical invaders were the Tuatha De Danann, a name which when translated from the Gaelic means The People of the Goddess Dana. Dana is identified with the Goddess Brigit, a very ancient 'mother' deity who was widely worshipped in Europe. Significantly, however, in Irish mythology she is recognized as having given birth to Ecne (pronounced Ec-nay), who is associated principally with 'poetry' (in its aspect as the spiritual embodiment of a divine art, of course).[32] Thus in conformity with the definitive principles that are to be found underlying the mythologies of every race, where quite naturally the mother goddess comes before her son, in Ireland we have Dana, or

Brigit, as the mother of the first or the highest god as well. But here in ancient Ireland we can see how this son or Sun-god is revealed in his most spiritually sophisticated aspect as being none other than the Sun-Logos or the divine Word. Here the god, Ecne, becomes poetry itself to the spiritual consciousness of these people, thus also highlighting how this art of poetry is regarded as the highest form of expression of the Word.

Later when the so-called Celts begin to 'invade' Ireland in approximately the 5th century B.C. they easily absorbed into their own culture the existing deities of this ancient Druidic civilization. (Indeed, this receptivity and spiritual flexibility of the Celts was the secret hallmark of their successful expansions everywhere in Europe around this time.)

The Celts, in other words, had a very marked spiritual magnanimity which allowed them to meet other cultures with an openness and a gesture of welcoming, especially if they felt these influences to be good and in accord with the betterment of their people generally.

When they came to Ireland they thus had no difficulty in absorbing into their own ways the mythic, cultural and spiritual influences at work there. And so it was that later when Christianity began to take root in Celtic Ireland, the ancient mother goddess Brigit or Dana, who still lived vividly in the mythic consciousness of the people, found her way easily into the new consciousness being wrought through Christianity. Eventually via this incarnational consciousness she came even to be identified with a real flesh and blood woman. This was no ordinary woman, of course, but a quite extraordinary one. And she came from Co. Kildare, near the middle or heart of the island.

ST. BRIGID OF KILDARE

Given the still very rich mythic consciousness of the time and place in which she lived and grew up, very little is known for certain (from an historical point of view) about this 'real' Brigid, apart from the approximate year of her death, which was between 523 and 525 A.D.

The chronic myth-making appetite of the Irish has left us little regarding Brigid in the way of those much (perhaps too much!) valued commodities of our own day – hard facts. However, the abundance of stories and legends about this early Christian saint does more than make up for this lack. Moreover, it is a situation which stimulates us into using our imagination and in this way perhaps to form an even more appropriate picture of Brigid than one built merely out of hard and dry facts. We can picture a woman inspired to the hilt with the fiercely independent spirit of the new Christian path, a woman deeply empowered, certainly, so as to enable her to work many marvels and wonders in the name of the great new God as she went about the country baptising and preaching the Good News in her own extraordinary and richly feminine way. In all of this, what she was surely most anxious to do was to try to wean her (especially male) contemporaries away from their all too war-loving way of life, while at the same time remaining, because of her ancestral background, deeply sympathetic to, and understanding of, their own pagan spiritual orientation.

Unlike the Romanized British-man, Patrick, who was actually her contemporary in this great missionary work, Brigid's background was purely Hiberno-Celtic and her upbringing, as indicated in the medieval hagiographic 'Life of Brigid' in the *Book of Lismore*, was given over to one of the initiates (Druids) of the old pagan religion, a caste which still flourished during her lifetime. To these Druids, a class of individuals who, as we have seen, were capable of a clairvoyant perception of the Incarnation, this spiritually fired virgin of Christ must indeed have been quite a force to be reckoned with! Furthermore, they must have clearly understood her destiny and have taken great care to stimulate, nourish, and to so refine her spiritual faculties for her to become a primary vehicle through which the Christian purification of the soul of the nation could take place.

As her fame and renown grew and stories of her miracle-workings spread far and wide through the land, this woman, in the simple minds of her people, soon became the live focus of a new type of consciousness that was being forced, precisely because of the implications of the Incarnation, to shift away from its age-old functioning through symbol and myth towards one concerned principally with the tangible and actual events and things of everyday life. Thus memories, thoughts, feelings, and all of those psychic and psychological faculties that were formerly only or mainly directed towards myths, the gods and so on, were now beginning to be given over to historical realities, so that this Brigid – once her great virtues and deeds became well known – not surprisingly grew in stature to such a degree that she became, with the passing of time, a semi-divine figure. Eventually she acquired the status in the imaginations of the people of nothing less than the foster-mother of God, i.e. of Christ himself![33] Indeed, in the 'Life of Brigid' she is referred to as none other than the 'Mary of the Gael.' However, from the point of view of our investigations here in this book, we may regard her in the light of Sophia or the divine Sophia Mystery.

For it is only this Sophia aspect of Brigid which will fully and clearly reveal, if properly investigated and understood, the mystery of the incarnational Spirit and the way it worked (and works!) in Ireland, which was, and is, fundamentally an inward, free, and essentially esoteric way. In Ireland, however, this inwardness was, paradoxically, as much to be found and cultivated in the beauty and expanse of nature as in the free-soaring spirit of the individual man or woman as he or she built up his or her new Christian relationship with the gods – now called angels – and the angelic world. And it is in this sense that it can be said that Nature herself, seen through this Christianized and angelic spirit-vision, was here regarded as the very temple of God. The Mystery temple-wisdom of the ancients, however, always gave the feminine Sophia aspect of their Trinitarian Godhead equal status with the Father and Son aspects, and this wisdom too was fully at work in the old pre-Celtic, Irish religion.

In this way we can come perhaps a little nearer to understanding how the esoteric Mystery spirit of Christianity worked its way so profoundly into the soul and spirit-religion of the Irish through the Druids and their disciples, one of whom was Brigid. Of this revered 'Mary of the Gael' we very revealingly read in the devotional biographic 'Life of Brigid' that 'Her name among created things is Dove', the dove being, as we have earlier pointed out, the most ancient of all symbols for the Sophia spirit.

THE CELTIC TRINITY

In trying to give expression to what is most essential to an understanding of Esoteric Christianity we have by now hopefully established quite clearly its trinitarian foundation. It is this more than any other aspect regarding the Divinity which holds the key to penetrating the deepest mysteries of God, man, and the universe. This 'secret' was well known also to the Celts long before they arrived in Ireland where they found it to be a well-established foundation of the much more ancient druidic culture and religion. The mythology of these continental Celts is full of references to a triune god. Indeed, there is in Klagenfurt in Austria (an ancient Celtic stronghold) a statue of a triune god, one component of which is pointedly feminine in gender, as it has breasts. And this symbiotic relationship between the Celts' own and the existing druidic culture which they found flourishing when they arrived in Ireland around the 5th or 6th century B.C. undoubtedly contributed much to the harmonious atmosphere which prevailed there some centuries later during the vital transitional period of Christianization.

It is therefore not surprising that, deeply associated with the legendary stories about how St. Patrick 'converted' the Irish, we have the symbol of the trefoil, or the tiny, difficult to find clover-type plant called the shamrock.

This Trinitarian foundation of consciousness, though lost

to, or actually banished from, formal Christian teaching and learning for a long time now, has nevertheless maintained at least an outward presence in modern Ireland. For the shamrock has, quite significantly, become the famous national emblem of the country.

However, in trying to characterize the most revealing tenets particular to this early Irish Christianity, one, more than all other aspects, is most apparent. That is how these two ancient historical figures, Patrick and Brigid, stand at the head of it, almost like a father and a mother at the head of a large family. It is also quite pertinent to note that these two complimentary figures, as archetypes, are still very much alive in the psyches of the Irish. In many ways, they can be looked upon as Celtic representatives of that necessary gender balance which must be sought for and achieved in the human soul if it aspires to a genuine and a strong faith, something for which the Irish have always been noted.

This is still undoubtedly the case, though it is a faith that will of necessity take a different form as time passes.

SAINT PATRICK

Patrick and Brigid were, roughly speaking, contemporaries. Of the two, however, it was St. Brigid who struck deepest into the soul of the nation, partly due no doubt to her mythic associations with the ancient goddess, but also very much due to the spiritual/religious jurisdiction she gained in the country because of her inspired missionary activity. In fact, there is evidence in the records of the early Irish Church indicating that at this time there were two quite distinct 'sees' in the country, one ascribed to Brigid and another to Patrick. The ancient Book of Armagh, for instance, records in a missive to her that her 'own province will be left completely under your sway' while outside of there, to the east and west, was deemed to be Patrick's domain.

In this controversy in the early Gaelic Church we can see at work the polarisation of two very distinct tendencies in the manner in which evangelization was actually taking place in Ireland. On the one hand, there was the ancient druidic wisdom-culture, the Christianization of which was embodied in Brigid, a development which may be termed *sophianic*. On the other hand, there was the Roman-type influence, essentially male and ecclesiastical in character, embodied in the work of Patrick, and which may be called *patristic*. It was in the careful marrying of these two complementary but potentially opposing powers that the strength of the early Irish Church lay. Furthermore, given the depth of power which they possess to stir the human soul, the benign and pacifying manner in which the resolution of these potentially conflicting tendencies was effected is testimony enough to the presence of the Spirit of the Holy Sophia in this early Irish Celtic Church.

Patrick, of course, is a much more historical figure than Brigid. There are many reasons for this. But perhaps the main one is that some of his own writings have survived. Moreover, they have managed to survive unsullied through all the burnings, pillaging and literary forgings that are so characteristic of our Western spiritual history. Perhaps their 'simple', unlearned, and unpretentious nature helped in this somewhat miraculous escape! In any event, they are there for us now and are in wide circulation, allowing us to easily examine them with much profit regarding just who this amazing man was and what he was about. We are able to look at Patrick, in other words, stripped of all the artificial legends and myths that were put out about him by the Roman Catholic Church for its own severely restricted purposes.

For nothing, after all, contributes more to giving a man real flesh and blood than his very own words!

By far the most interesting and revealing of these writings is the one known as the Confession, undisputedly attributed by scholars to Patrick's own hand. Whereas a lot of what was later written by 'churched' scribes and hagiographers about Patrick (and about the saints generally) tends to come more out of fantasy and imagination than reality, in Patrick's own Confession the real man of flesh and blood, in all his human weakness as well as in his undeniable virtue, piety and saintliness, comes across very clearly. Moreover, in reading his Confession we can gain for ourselves some of those much sought-after items indispensable in the pursuit of any discipline, spiritual or otherwise, i.e. concrete facts.

Thus we know for certain that as a boy Patrick was abducted from his home in Britain during one of the on-going slave and cattle raids that the Irish made upon her big neighbouring island in those far-off days. He was sixteen at the time. He was subsequently sold to one who (legend has it) was a Druid. So here at this impressionable age we have a young man who was suddenly and violently wrenched from the (comparatively speaking) civilized and cultured life of his Roman Christian upbringing, one where his father held the privileged position of a deacon in the Church of the period. In this providential way our Patrick was thrust deep into that misty and forbidden land to the west, a land so brim-full of myth, magic, and wonder that no boy could possibly have been there for any length of time without becoming deeply and permanently touched by the experience. Patrick was in Ireland, he tells us, for six long years, all of this time with the one man whom he served as a slave and a shepherd.

Though Patrick does not say it explicitly, we can easily imagine this wise master of his becoming very aware of his boy's simple and developing piety, and in this would have undoubtedly encouraged him. Furthermore, though not necessarily Christian, the Druid master would surely have taught and shown Patrick many things through which he could learn to stimulate his intuition, strengthen his imagination, and thus spiritually nourish his tender and growing Christian soul. Though it was certainly a hard life for the young Patrick as he clearly indicates, it was also one that was full of mystery and enchantment as the manner and content of his Confession also very convincingly reveals.

Having thus become well acquainted with this strange land, its sophisticated religion, its seasonal customs, and its spiritually inclined people, Patrick was able to thoroughly cultivate the Christian virtues he had heard about in his boyhood schooling. Especially he practised modesty and piety, and also became very accomplished, he tells us, in the valuable and subtle arts of prayer and meditation. In this way he was gradually awakened to the wonderful reality of God and to his own higher and guardian angelic being. Not surprisingly he was therefore led eventually, he tells us, by the medium of a prophetic dream, to a ship in which he would, with great joy, escape his slavery.

PATRICK'S DREAM

What happens next provides us with a very deep insight indeed into the manner of Patrick's full initiation into, or confirmation of, his Christian baptism. This also took the form of a kind of visionary dream. In his recounting of this episode we see very clearly at work in the young man's psyche the influence of the ancient Sun-wisdom, so vitally and vibrantly cultivated within the druidic and gradually Christianizing traditions of Hibernia, much of which Patrick had absorbed during his six years of slavery.

On the ship taking him away from Ireland, Patrick tell us, 'I was sleeping and Satan tempted me powerfully, which will be a memory as long as I am in this body, and he fell on me like a great rock while nothing in my limbs had any strength. But how did it occur to me in my ignorance to call upon Helias? And meantime I saw the Sun rise in the sky, and while I shouted Helia, Helia, with all my might, lo and behold the splendour of that Sun fell down on me and at once smashed off all the weight from me, and I believe I was helped by Christ my Lord.'

Helios is of course another name for the ancient Sun god, Apollo or Phoebus. (The slightly different spelling can easily be put down to Patrick's own use of the Latin which is widely recognized by modern scholars, and especially by Patrick himself, as being of a low standard.)

Later in his Confession Patrick reaffirms his deep

awareness of this Sun-nature of the Christ Being when he explicitly says, 'we shall rise in the brightness of the Sun, that is, in the glory of Christ Jesus our Redeemer.'

Furthermore, in a vision he had a number of years after he left Ireland, he indicates even more clearly how deeply his soul had become infused with the Sun-Spirit as it manifested itself so powerfully in its Solar Logos or Word aspect in Hibernia: 'And there I saw in the night the vision of a man whose name was Victoricus, coming as it were from Ireland with countless letters. And he gave me one of them and I read the opening words of the letter which were: "The voice of the Irish." And as I read the beginning of the letter I thought at the same moment I head their voice – they were those beside the Wood of Volclut, which is near the western sea – and thus did they cry out as with one mouth: "We ask thee, boy, come walk among us once more." '

Immediately after this account of his vision Patrick says that in another dream the Irish spoke to him as if they were the very mouth of Christ himself!

We can be left with no doubt, therefore, of how deeply connected Patrick felt the Sun Logos and the island and people of Ireland to be.

Through his dreams, his visions and his intuitions, as well as in many other ways, Patrick's enchantment with Hibernia gradually matured into a religious and spiritual conviction of the very highest order, and so he promised Christ he would return to the Irish to establish more firmly the Word of God there. After overcoming great obstacles placed in his path by some of his clerical associates in the Roman Catholic Church, who doubtless envied or were suspicious of his humble yet great and wilful spiritual strength and energy, he was eventually made bishop and came to Ireland with the authority of the established orthodoxy. His ostensible mission was to bring some kind of ecclesiastical order to the Christians in Ireland, which he duly did. However, he was so fired by the spiritual sunlight of the Sophia-Christ that he powerfully extended the parameters of the Gospel's influence greatly by penetrating with it, through unceasing toil and effort, into every nook and cranny of the (often very difficult to negotiate) terrain.

PELAGIUS AND THE ANCIENT WISDOM

Patrick did astounding and marvellous work for the Gospel in Ireland. There is no doubt whatever about this. But in attempting to make a true assessment of his place, not only in the history of the Irish Church, but also in the whole strange development of the spirit within the wider Church itself, we must now consider the life and work of another man, one who was Patrick's contemporary, and who can be regarded in many ways as much more complementary to Brigid than Patrick himself. This was Pelagius.

Pelagius shot like a bolt of spiritual lightening out of the far western twilit world and into the limelight of busy and important Church affairs in Rome towards the very end of the 4th century. This big, strong, rough-featured Celtic holy man must surely have cut a strange figure in the dying and shabby grandeur of the decadent Roman culture of the period. He was proffering a brand of Christianity that was fully matured, light-filled, and at once freely, eloquently, and convincingly articulated, yet also totally at odds with the centralist and theocratic designs of the increasingly

Roman-influenced orthodoxy. Pelagius's free Celtic expression of the incarnational spirit was far too pure and strong for the dogmatic type of theologians emerging in the Roman Church at this time, of whom St. Augustine is by far the best known.

They called him Pelagius because this name was a Greek rendering of the Celtic appellative 'morgan' meaning 'sea-born' or 'from over the sea', and without any deliberate intention of creating a school or encouraging an organized following for his beliefs, this man soon began to attract a growing numbers of followers.

Pelagius was a product of that period of pre-patristic Irish Christianity about which, apart from Pelagius himself, very little is known. Nevertheless, from this one highly influential and colourful exponent of it we can gain a good appreciation and understanding of the spiritual depth and richness of the transitional and increasingly Christianized culture in Ireland at this time.

That Pelagius was from Ireland need hardly be doubted. For although he was nicknamed 'Brito' by his prime opponent St. Augustine, this need hardly be taken as a true indication of his origin, which it often has been. A 'Brito' may indeed have been one from 'over the sea' (i.e. from Britain), but in those far-off days the whole of the British Isles was lumped together in the minds of most people. And St. Jerome, perhaps *the* most learned of all of the Latin Church Fathers, plainly calls Pelagius 'of Irish race, from the region of Britain'.

By the time Pelagius had arrived on the scene, the western Roman Church was becoming ever more hierarchical in its style, and freedom-denying in its spirit.

The light of The Gnosis had by this time been well and truly quenched, and the ultimate defeat of that other great 'heresy' of the early Church, Arianism, was well under way. The hardening and expanding triumphalism resulting from these victories had to have its 'theorizers', of course, and even more importantly, its 'theologisers'. And in St. Augustine of Hippo (354 – 430) we have the most eloquent, prolific, and convincing protagonist of this emerging trend in the early Church. It is a trend nevertheless that can hardly be seen in any other light than that of a gathering of the forces of darkness, for it was essentially to do with the denying of the freedom of the individual human spirit. It was thus also and inevitably a trend that, in its psychology and theology, was centred far more on death than on resurrection. Augustine's troubled life and the negative brand of theology that it produced was so thoroughly shaped by and steeped in sensual remorse, the darkness of sin, and the burden of guilt, that he would probably have needed another rebirth, in addition to the one he speaks about in his *Confession*, if he were to truly see the light of the Sun-spirit that was shining so purely through this holy and freedom-loving Celtic sage, Pelagius.

St. Augustine, however, was rightly very highly regarded for the eloquent manner in which he could define and articulate a basis for a real and solid *faith* in Christ, something moreover the Church simply had to learn to do if it was going to succeed in a world where many gods vied for the people's simple faith. One can thus say in a sense that the Church was adopting a policy of 'faith at any price'. To gain this depth of faith however, the price demanded was a relinquishing of the true soaring spirit of knowledge and wisdom.

Pelagius's theology of the free spirit had no place in such a half-baked scheme, and it is not surprising that this free ambassador of the Christianised Mystery-wisdom of the Sophia spirit would get branded quickly as a despised 'heretic.'

The whole furore in the early Church surrounding this Irishman and his great wisdom, i.e. the Pelagian heresy, and the manner in which Pelagius himself became anathematized through it, was one upon which the Church of Rome, as distinct from the still broadly unified universal Church of Christ, thoroughly sharpened its dogmatic and power-hungry teeth. Up to this point there had been as yet no clear division between the Eastern, Western, or indeed any other 'see' of the Church. The concept of the one and only 'Holy See' had not been invoked. When the controversy between Augustine and Pelagius reached its climax, however (and significantly this came only *after* the Eastern bishops *in collegium* had refused to anathematize Pelagius!), the highly influential Augustine took the decisive step of honouring the Bishop of Rome with a request for him to personally, officially, and finally adjudicate on the matter of Pelagius! Innocent the First, needless to say, jumped at the opportunity to strengthen his own hand regarding his ambitions for Rome, sided with Augustine, and quickly denounced Pelagius. This was a very decisive moment in the history of the Western Church, for from then on the Bishop of Rome gradually established and strengthened his centralist power structure and became known and duly recognized as the Pope of this Petrine Church.

In this manner Pelagius, the great early Irish exponent of a free logosophical or Johannine Christianity, vanishes from the scene even more suddenly than he arrived, for no trace whatsoever of him has come to light after this time. The only legitimate picture one can form of this sorry episode in the Church is that of yet another bright-shining and living spirit-light being simply snuffed out! Needless to say, however, Pelagius's influence, like that of Arius and other 'heretics' and free spirit-lovers before him, continued for a long time afterwards.

We can thus see that already by Patrick's time the Celtic Church had reached a very high degree of cultural and free spiritual/religious sophistication. Pelagius himself is a fine testimony to this. We can tell that his wisdom and learning was at once ancient, forward-looking and eclectic. We know that his consciousness would have been infused and informed with the Mystery and mythic wisdom of his druidic/Celtic forebears. He had this ancient cosmic awareness and would by dint of it have cultivated knowledge of the being and beings of the planets and the stars, i.e. of the gods as such. However, Pelagius achieved his high status because he was also highly learned in the progressive and civilizing disciplines of his own day. He would not have been able to go to Rome or elsewhere as a missionary if he did not have these qualifications. He spoke Greek and Latin (and probably even Hebrew) fluently, and though little of his written work survived the inevitable book-burnings which followed in the wake of his branding as a heretic, from what is available, his thought and teaching can be discerned.

In any informed and genuine history of the logosophical

spirit as it manifested within the body of Christianity, something which we are of course here attempting, the part played by the early Hiberno-Celtic Church should be pivotal. By understanding both the nature and the manifestation of this spirit in Ireland, and by clearly recognizing it as both the foundation stone and the driving force at the heart of this unique Christo-Celtic culture, we are able to see it fully, vitally, and productively at work in the world as it was originally intended to be by its founder. Not only that, but we are also able to see, by learning something of the manner in which this high spiritual culture was purposely and ignorantly terminated, how the spirit itself failed to penetrate the Western Church to any significant degree after this dismal termination. This failure was directly linked to the successful incorporation of the unorthodox but spiritually imbued free Celtic Church into the dry Roman orthodoxy and its largely temporal, dogmatic, and law-ridden agenda.

The sending of Patrick to Ireland was the first step in this direction. Patrick, however, was very much his own man, and his influence, despite his Roman background, can only be regarded as positive for the overall development of Gaelic Christianity. The manner therefore in which the Roman orthodoxy managed eventually to kill off the Christo-Celtic sprit came about in a different way, and to this we shall now turn our attention.

CHAPTER EIGHT

TO HELL OR TO ROME!

In order to fully understand and appreciate how the demise of the Celtic Church spelled the virtual end of a true and genuine spirituality within the body of western Christianity, we must know that the chief characteristic of the spirit of this Celtic Church was the essential *freedom* of its expression, something which was in total opposition to the Roman outlook.

But what in effect did this mean? In a nutshell, it meant that the Celtic Church affirmed, with the deepest possible trust, faith in, and love of Christ, that each man or woman can come to know God, overcome sin and so on through the power of his or her own unique and spiritually imbued *free will*. The pure and esoteric inwardness of the working of the Holy Spirit in man was therefore fully and unambiguously upheld. Thus the whole edifice, structure, and culture of the Celtic Church, all of that which naturally and organically followed upon this prime realization and its implications, was totally different from, and completely at odds with, the orthodox position upheld by Rome. For conventional Roman theology was now busily inculcating the doctrine into the minds and hearts of its flock that a man or a woman can only come to God by being told how to do so by someone else! In effect this meant, of course, *us* in Rome. Blind faith for the masses, yes! Inspired knowledge, no!

Simply put, this was the foundation-stone of Rome's theocracy. If there is to be any dispute at all about knowledge from now on, we in Rome will decide about it, full stop! The divine, faithful, trusting, and inwardly renewing grace of the individual's own higher angelic being, i.e. his true and deepest spirit Self, was quite simply not recognized by the outward-looking and temporally influenced Roman Church. The public disputes which took place at this time between the Celtic Church and Rome about the true date of Easter, about how to cut your hair properly (the tonsure) and all the rest of it, were merely spurious or political 'red herrings' designed to bring the Irish into a Roman line of thinking. And it was merely a matter of time, given the sort of political backing which Rome had, and which it was busily consolidating, before it fully had its way.

Even in the old pre-Christian Roman world there was virtually no feeling for, or understanding of, the ancient Mystery wisdom upon which most of the religions, cultures, and civic societies of antiquity had been built. This would have been most especially true for the Romans regarding that mystery-filled and strange land far away to the twilit west, Hibernia. Rome was probably unique in respect of its being the only city and culture of antiquity which was not founded upon, or inspired in some way, by the initiatory insights of the ancient Mystery temple-wisdom. In fact, quite the reverse was the case. The impulse for this Roman civilization arose fundamentally out of an exploitation of those very vacuous psychic forces which, ordinarily under the tight control of benign initiates and their disciples, spread out indiscriminately all over the world only to be harnessed by evil-minded men.

Let us digress here a little and look at this matter briefly, for it is important to an understanding of the brutish and hard nature of this Roman consciousness.

ROME AND THE BEAST

Traditionally the city of Rome was founded in the year 753 B.C. and from her very beginnings she set her face resolutely against the prophetic, the spiritual, and the cosmic, against all those forces inherent in the truly human form, the cultivation of which had been of the very essence of the work and teaching of the Mystery temples. Even worse, this Roman creation proceeded to twist whatever base spiritual power she could derive from what was left of these Mysteries into serving her very imperialistic, militaristic, and materialistic ends. The Roman culture was thus highly synthetic and artificial in nature, and thoroughly unoriginal in character, having no natural or indigenous source of spiritual nourishment which, as a matter of course, sustained former cultures out of the richness of their own temples and initiates – all of which helps to account for the hideous institutionalization of mass-murder, cruelty and butchery which lay at Rome's very centre, and which were the focus of its chief cultural ceremonies and civic trappings.

If we wish to try to gain some understanding of just where all such bestiality could possibly have originated from, the situation is really very well illustrated by the fact that the only true or purely Roman god, i.e. a god who does not have a counterpart or a precursor in any other pantheon, is the one they named Janus, who apart from being their *one supreme god* was also a god with *two* heads (the apotheosis, you could say, of confusion, divisiveness, and even of psychosis!). And he was always, very revealingly, placed at the doorway of their temples, looking both ways. Hence the significant and defiant gesture of looking into the temple to loot what he could . . . before moving off to the next one!

Rome, in other words, epitomizes this turning away from the ancient starry wisdom of the gods in the heavens, and sets her narrow eyes greedily and angrily upon the hard earth itself for the purpose, primarily, of looting and little else. She essentially represented a denial of the cosmic warmth of the Sophia spirit, and brazenly and ignorantly tries to twist this spirit around by turning man himself, in his purely materialistic aspect, into a god. We have here, in all of this, a sort of deification of the material, something which is nothing less than a perversion of the truth of the ancient wisdom. It was inevitable, therefore, that the embodiment of a spirit such as this, i.e. Caesar, would in the end arrogantly declare himself to be a god!

We can thus see that Rome was founded upon and built

up out of those dubious forces and strengths indicative of
man's lower nature: those angers, passions, desires, and
turbulent emotions, all of which it is the business of true
spirituality and true religion to subdue and tame, but
certainly not to exploit for political or indeed any other
purpose. The French author and initiate, Edouard Schuré,
who had an encyclopaedic knowledge of the ancient
wisdom and ancient cultures generally, characterized the
situation thus:

> *What is Rome's origin? The conjuration of a greedy
> oligarchy in the name of brute force; the oppression
> of human intellect, of religion, science and art
> through deified political power; in other words the
> opposite of truth according to which a government
> draws its power only from the supreme principles of
> science, justice and economy. All Roman history is
> but the outgrowth of this pact of iniquity by which
> the Roman senators declared war first on Italy and
> then on the human race. They chose their symbol
> well! The brass She-Wolf, raising her wild hair and
> moving her hyena-head on the Capitoline, is the
> reflection of the government, the demon which will
> possess the Roman soul to the very last.*[34]

When the light of the Mystery wisdom, which had been so
powerfully renewed through the Incarnation, eventually
became consolidated to some degree in the Roman world,
given the background just outlined it was inevitable that it
would not be met there with the same understanding and
appreciation that it met with in other places, especially

Ireland. The Christo-Celtic culture which flowered in Ireland was, as we have seen, a direct outcome of the Hibernian Mysteries. It was a remarkably pure, perhaps a unique spiritual culture, and this was probably due to the fact that unlike all of the other ancient Mysteries, these Hibernian Mysteries had not become corrupted. They had merely withdrawn, and taking note of the gathering darkness brought down upon the world by the madness of Rome, became ever more careful, secretive, and esoteric in their working.

The spiritual perception of the Christ Being thus available within the framework of this Irish culture was infinitely more inward, ethereal, and profound than that which could be had in any other, especially Roman-influenced, culture. It was also in Ireland that a manifestly simple and humble expression of this spirit which took place (humility being, after all, the hallmark of all true and genuine spirituality). Inevitably, therefore, the outer, cultic forms of the new religion also took on a relatively simple mode of expression. For instance, the physical churches themselves, if and when they were built at all, were nearly always small, simple, made of wood, and rarely of stone (and only then in places where wood would not withstand the harsh weather). The people regularly worshipped out of doors amidst the beauty of their natural surroundings and gathered devoutly around their exquisite high stone Sun-crosses which were often erected in places known from time immemorial to have been receptive to the spiritual vibrations entering the atmosphere of the Earth from the cosmos.

An echo of the dignified, profound, ethereal, yet simple Christ-consciousness of these early Irish followers of the new Way can be found in the prayers and blessings which they used, some of which have survived from this time. These prayers and blessings are full of a wondrous and heartfelt expression of the love and beauty that shines out from the Christ-imbued natural world and hint to us of the deep spiritual treasures of the Celtic Church.

THANKSGIVING[35]

Thanks to Thee, O God, that I have risen today,
To the rising of this life itself;
May it be to Thine own glory, O God of every gift,
And to the glory of my soul likewise.

O great God, aid Thou my soul
With the aiding of Thine own mercy;
Even as I clothe my body with wool,
Cover Thou my soul with the shadow of Thy wing.

Help me to avoid every sin,
And the source of every sin to forsake;
And as the mist scatters on the crest of the hills,
May each ill haze clear from my soul, O God.

In an environment where a spiritually imbued consciousness is nurtured such as the one capable of producing hymns and prayers like this, structures and organizations fall naturally into their proper place. There is no need here of dogmatic and rigid codes of practice and structural methods stringently enforced. To the hard, narrow, gaze of the Roman eye, however, the simplicity and profound spirituality of the Celtic Church was nothing but backwardness, rusticity, and paganism.

Worse still, it became ever more in their eyes a harbinger of that dreaded and demonized individual, the heretic.

ROME AND IRELAND

The Pelagian controversy undoubtedly stirred the whole Roman Christian world into deep suspicion of what was going on in Ireland. Patrick, of course, because of his intimate knowledge of the Irish people, coupled with the perspective he had gained from his wider worldly experience, knew deep in his heart what the Irish wanted and needed. Through this, in his own inspired way, he wished to help them awaken to an even stronger sense of community in Christ than they already possessed. Rome, however, had a very different agenda.

The Pelagian controversy had preceded Patrick's arrival in Ireland by only a short number of years, and as such, it must have had a strong bearing upon the pending question of Patrick's proposed mission. Certain reactionary forces were thus aroused within the Church against Patrick, for they feared he would not be able to forward Rome's agenda properly. As Patrick himself so painfully recalls in his *Confession*, the most insidious types of obstacles were placed upon his path of gaining the proper authoritative blessings for his mission Ireland, an authority he reckoned he required if he was to properly execute his mission there.

Undoubtedly Patrick's whole demeanour, his background, his self-confessed 'rusticity', if not indeed his actual philosophical leanings, would, in the eyes of the emerging intellectual princes of the Roman Church, have very strongly smacked of the dreaded Pelagianism. Patrick therefore was both opposed and vilified as he tried to gain episcopal recognition for his proposed work. In this manner Patrick and his holy mission were side-lined, and Rome, in its ambitious plans to haul Ireland and the Celtic Church generally into the sphere of its ordered, ecclesiastical, but essentially temporal influence, sent someone else instead. He was someone whom they obviously felt could carry out their plans in a much more orthodox fashion. This man was called Palladius and he came to Ireland in the year 431.

Patrick was, needless to say, shattered to the very depths of this soul by this turn of events, for ever since he had left Ireland many years before, his whole life had been lived in a sort of preparation for going back to these people. His rejection was thus undoubtedly his own particular 'harrowing of hell', his very own experience of the Passion, for he indicated most sorrowfully in his Confession that he came very near to losing his Christian soul during this time of his severest testing.

Providence, however, was secretly at work in all of this and Patrick came through his period of testing an even stronger and more wilful servant of the Christ than he had already been. For Palladius died unexpectedly very soon after commencing his work in Ireland. This was a propitious and (for Patrick) a fortuitous event that enabled him very soon afterwards to obtain from his superiors the vital seal of approval for his hopes and plans. And so, in the year 432, Patrick began his great work for Christ, for the Gospel, and for the universal and free Church of God in the holy island of Ireland.

****

As we have said earlier, Christianity, right from its very inception, began to work spiritually within the very receptive vessel of the Irish folk-soul in quite a unique way. Furthermore, we have seen that this was essentially an inward or esoteric working, a phenomenon of which Patrick would have been only too well aware, having spent the most formative years of his youth there. He knew therefore that coercion should be used very sparingly. His mission, he was well aware, was far more concerned with *confirming*, or of harnessing the growing Christ-consciousness into a greater and more conscious, even national unity.

It has been authoritatively stated that Patrick brought Christianity to every corner of the island in the space of his 30 years work there. (He is reputed to have died in the year 461 and is buried together with Brigid and that other great early Irish saint, Columba, in Downpatrick, Co. Down.)

Patrick brought order into the Celtic Church. This was an ordering of which the thriving monastic settlement was the linchpin. It was a highly disciplined general society of closely interlinked spiritual *familia* communities where every branch of learning was assiduously cultivated, and was largely the outcome of Patrick's work in Ireland. Because such learning and spiritual activity penetrated and took hold of the country to such a large degree, the land eventually became known as the island of Saints and Scholars.

At a time when the rest of Europe was yielding to the turmoil of the 'barbarian invasions', Ireland in its sea-bound seclusion was providentially in a position to profit from this turmoil. Insofar as they could manage to reach the island, Ireland provided a safe haven for many a Christian scholar on the run from his ignorant, head-hunting, and blood-letting heathen contemporaries. Thus, into this slowly forming Christian vessel in old Hibernia, where a rich residue of the ancient druidic wisdom still prospered, there flowed the new Christian-inspired learning which had long been cultivated in the East and elsewhere.

All this helped to produce the diverse and spiritually imbued art and learning which has come to be known as the Celtic Church. It was indeed here in Ireland that the light of the Sophia-Christ in its Western configuration took hold fully, and here that this spirit was embraced so lovingly that it nurtured not only the already deeply spiritual qualities of the Irish soul herself, but also the folk-soul of Europe.

It was during these dark, barbaric years of European history that the precious Christ-light streamed out of Celtic Ireland and into Europe with those bands of missionary saints who, in this highly productive way, elected for the privilege of a Christian martyrdom. In doing so these saints and scholars managed heroically to keep alive, in an ever-darkening world, the great incarnational Mystery-spirit in its most essential characteristic, that of freedom.

THE ONE TRUE CHURCH?

We speak now of the 5th to 8th centuries, which is the approximate duration of what is generally regarded as the Gaelic or Celtic Church. This was also precisely the period when the Roman Church was busily attempting to consolidate in various ways its own peculiar and unilateral claim to be the 'one true Church.' In its limited vision, however, Rome, on the continent, tended to lump the Irish in with everyone else who got in its way and who were simply put down as 'heathens'. This was a blatant error and one committed to the ultimate detriment of the spirit of the truly universal Church.

In their work to Christianise Europe at this time, the Irish were far more tolerant of, and sympathetic to, the old customs and rites of the ancient worship which inevitably still lingered on within the migrating tribes, echoing their own diverse and particular Mystery streams. Rome, however, had totally different, totally opposite methods to the Irish in the handling of these delicate areas of evangelical activity. Because of the tolerance of the Irish in this and other aspects of their missionary activity, they were very widely respected and much sought after by intelligent leaders and rulers as being capable of injecting a much-needed civilizing, pacifying, and benign influence into the more robust practices and warlike psychology of many of these tribal groupings under their jurisdiction. The Irish, however, then became, because of their apparently 'soft' approach, an easy target for the Roman, legalistic, and conforming bias to focus upon. Thus, in their religious politicking and spiritual propaganda they proceeded to anathematize the Irish right, left, and centre.

It is in the person of St. Boniface (657 – 754), who appears on the scene at this time, that the whole approach of Rome finds its most energetic, coercive, and fanatical expression. Although this English saint is widely recognized and eulogized in conventional accounts of European and Church history as the "Apostle to the

Germans", 'detailed knowledge of his work reveals that he was less a converter of the heathen than a commissioner with the task of bringing into the Roman Church those regions on the mainland [of Europe] which had been Christianized by the Irish'.[36]

Boniface went about his work in very steadfast ways, many of which have the hallmark of the true fanatic. For instance, one of his chief methods of evangelization was the ruthless destruction of traditional places of worship! Brazenly daring the pagans and their gods by virtue of his zeal for Christ and his thirst for power, this Boniface was Pope Gregory's prime emissary in the continuation of the Romanizing of the Church which his predecessor, the very powerful first Gregory (the Great) had, about a century before, so resolutely shifted into top gear.

ROME ABHORS THE CELTIC SUN-WISDOM

In the conflict between Boniface and the Irishman Virgilius (Fergil), who was made Bishop of Salzburg around this time, we have a good example of both the spiritual shallowness of the Roman Church and its methods, and the fanaticism which this inevitably bred. Because Virgilius was an exponent of the Christo-Celtic Mystery wisdom of Ireland, he was privy to much astronomical/astrological information of which the Romans not only knew nothing, but actually cared about even less. The fabulous Sun wisdom of the Celts represented little more to the Romans than merely a confirmation of that criminalizing label which they were so wont to use to classify all those who did not toe the dogmatic line – pagans, in other words. This Celtic wisdom was nevertheless something which, because of its Sun and star nature, was capable of producing true scientific knowledge and insights into the Earth and its relationship to the cosmos, and it could thus put forward ideas which were very advanced for their time. It is evident from this conflict between Boniface and Fergil that the Irish already had, at this early time, very advanced astronomical concepts.

Fergil could show, for instance, even in the 8th century, to the total bewilderment of the Romans, that the Sun and the Moon could exist not only above the Earth but below it also. The Romans, however, had no wish to look up to the Sun, Moon, planets, and stars, and seek in them the spiritual/scientific language of the Celts. Moreover, it was this kind of thing that most galled them! The new breed of Catholic doctrine makers wanted to know nothing whatsoever about the planets, the stars, and the cosmos. Thus, understandably, Boniface was furious when this 'heathen' Fergil was made Bishop of Salzburg and wanted to be rid of him as quickly as possible!

In setting about his work of Romanization, Boniface was resolute: he solicited no less a personage than the Pope himself. He apparently *had* to go to this extreme, for Fergil was not to be so easily got rid of! Indeed, Fergil obviously stood in very high esteem with many high-ranking people of the secular world at this time and had even secured the Bishopric of Salzburg's high recommendation through the Frankish King, Peppin the Short. Notwithstanding this, Pope Zacharias threw his full support behind Boniface, for he was full of admiration for him and in total agreement with his methods of Romanization. He thus wrote to Boniface, saying:

> *This Virgilius [Fergil] was found guilty by you of deviating from Catholic doctrine. If it is established that in his opinion there is yet another world and other human beings under the Earth, and there is another Sun and Moon, you are to hold a Church assembly and drive him out of the Church, after you have stripped him of his priestly status.*[37]

Zacharias went on to say that Fergil then should be arrested and brought to Rome and there charged with heresy!

Apart from anything else, this episode is indicative of the strength and depth of the Irish spiritual wisdom by virtue of the very fact of Virgilius's surviving this systematic programme of vilification. For survive he did! Moreover, he 'remained until his death in 784 a brilliant embodiment of the free Irish school of thought'.[38]

Boniface alas met with perhaps a more predictable end! In 754 he and a band of his converts were set upon and unceremoniously massacred by an army of deeply offended 'heathens' in the region of West Friesland!

THE DECLINE OF THE CELTIC CHURCH

What has been called the Golden Age of the Celtic Church was quite a short period, approximately the duration of the 6th century. It is indeed an Age so short that when one evaluates its contribution to the long-term civilizing of Europe, its very brevity is evidence of the quality, depth, and intensity of its spirituality.

But already by the middle of the 7th century Rome saw fit to call a general Synod in England, the chief objective of which was to curb the activities of the Irish monks, and undoubtedly also to indirectly begin what it surely considered it's much more important work, that of the complete Romanization of the Island of Saints and Scholars. The Church assembly we here speak of is the famous Synod of Whitby which was held in the year 664, an event which historically marks the beginning of the end of the free Gaelic Church. It was from this event onwards that Rome, by cleverly manipulating its existing claims to authority, obtained substantive agreement, despite Irish objections, regarding the method of fixing Easter Sunday in the Church calendar. By virtue of gaining victory in this, as well as in other minor matters at the Synod, Rome was able gradually to suppress the esoteric spirit at work within the Celtic soul and subsequently impose its authoritative, centralist, and dogmatic kind of ecclesiastical control over the evolving church in Ireland.

But quite apart from this action by the Roman Church there was another historical factor which sounded the death-knell of the free Celtic spirit.

Although Ireland had escaped the grip of Roman imperialism in earlier times and subsequently (primarily because of her isolated situation) also had escaped the cultural and civic upheavals resulting from the 'barbarian invasions' during the break-up of the Empire, Ireland's time of safe seclusion eventually came to an end. This began in the year 795 with the arrival of the first sinister shiploads of fighting-men from Scandinavia. These men, who were in truth the real terrorists of their time, were out to impose their crude will upon whomsoever provided them with the most lucrative spoils. And the island of Saints and Scholars was indeed a paradise of rich picking for them. These were the Vikings!

Over a period of a few centuries, these mobs of foreigners terrorized the quiet, deeply spiritual and pastoral land of Erin, killing, pillaging, looting and ransacking everything in sight. This especially applied to the monasteries, of course, which by this time housed most of the wealth worth talking about in the country. Throngs of holy monks and saints were massacred, and it was in this bloody and tragic manner that one of the greatest periods of Christian culture the world has yet known came to an end.

A spirit as strong as that which built and sustained this Celtic culture is, however, not one to be easily or, one suspects, ever entirely snuffed out. It is true that by the time of the Viking invasions the great missionary activity of the free Celtic Church in Europe was well and truly over anyway. But despite this decline, Ireland continued to be a place where knowledge of the true spirit of Sophia was capable of being systematically cultivated. Though we can have but little idea of the actual spiritual perceptions available to the people at large in such far-off times, it is obvious from what we *can* glean from an historical overview that the soul of the people of Ireland remained spiritually rich for a long time after the Roman Church began to tighten its dogmatic grip and squeeze out the Celtic Mystery spirit. And it is obvious also that something of this spirit survived even the systematic destruction by the Vikings.

From the rich tapestry of Gaelic story, legend, and

folklore we can get some idea of the depth of the soul and spiritual life of the people at this time of transition, and perhaps the best evidence for this emerges in the personality of one whose influence has reached far beyond the boundaries of his native land. This is the 9th century Irish scholar John Scotus Erigena, who is rightly regarded as one of the key figures capable of unlocking the whole confused and tragic history of our Western spirituality. At this vital time of his appearance, when the last rich and colourful remnants of the ancient cosmic wisdom were being flattened into the dark uniformity of Roman Catholic authoritarianism, this great individual emerged like a thunderbolt out of Ireland onto the European scene as a sort of philosophical saviour.

JOHN SCOTUS ERIGENA: SHAPER OF THE MIDDLE AGES

John Scotus Erigena acquired such a high status because he was expounding in his teachings and writings the self-same wisdom of the ancients, but a teaching and a wisdom that was now vitally renewed through the powerful spiritual Event of the Incarnation. Moreover, he was doing so at a time when Europe generally was in the very thick of its own darkest age and desperately in need of one such as him.

We arrive now at a time in Europe when its destiny can be seen in terms of a crucible wherein the Church, at whatever cost, was going to assert herself and carve out her place in the world amidst an ever-increasing awareness of the power of darkness and evil. It was, however, a time which in retrospect can also be seen to have a seed or womblike quality. Within it preparations were being made for the great cultural and spiritual renaissance which was soon to emerge and which would culminate in the achievements of the Middle Ages.

John Scotus Erigena was a key figure in this cultural and spiritual renaissance. His philosophical work can be viewed as fundamental to the foundations upon which this great period of our recent Western history and culture was laid, and which had as its central concept the remarkable one of 'Christendom'.

Needless to say, the web of political, spiritual, and psychological intrigues which played into the forming of this Age are complex in the extreme. We will therefore have to content ourselves here with merely highlighting some of the more salient features involved, and in so doing hopefully appreciate all the more readily the significance of Erigena. We should thus clearly recognize that we are now entering a time in Europe when the Church was penetrating ever more thoroughly into the lives of each and every individual and, more to the point, was doing so with a spiritual power which was based squarely on a blind, forcibly imposed acceptance of an incarnational faith in Jesus Christ. In such a circumstance it was only to be expected that the reasons for the Church's strange actions in this regard (and we need not bother to recount any of these here) had to be ever more carefully teased out and defined. It must be remembered that we are also entering a period of history when individual consciousness was very much on the rise; out of this, their very *self-recognition*, human beings were beginning to question themselves and the world in a way they had never done before.[39] Thus an intellectual backdrop, a movement even, was gradually emerging within this growing medieval culture which had the primary function of supplying the 'proofs of reason' for (especially) the Church's confusing, often irrational, and regularly immoral conduct. This is the movement we have come to know as Scholasticism.

Although he could not by any means be regarded as being in sympathy with Scholasticism as such, nevertheless insofar as the Church saw fit to cultivate a pure philosophy which it understandably regarded as being ultimately the only way in which it could manage to survive in the long-term as a cohesive religious entity in the world, John Scotus can be seen as the father of this philosophical movement. The fact that he was later branded as a heretic is evidence enough of the growing strength of the opposition within the orthodox Church to the logosophical (or, to put it more conventionally, the Johannine) spirit still lingering within it, something due chiefly to the Irish dimension, of which Erigena was the latest and perhaps the greatest spokesman.

Erigena's wisdom was of the very essence of the spirit of the divine Sophia, or Logos, to which his most celebrated work is the perfect witness. Let us therefore briefly consider it.

This short work is called *The Voice of the Eagle* and in it Erigena expounds upon the Prologue to the Gospel of St. John. Erigena takes these famous verses of the Gospel and uses them to articulate the depths of his own knowledge and wisdom, because it is in these verses, he was only too well aware, that the Gospel is proclaimed in all its spiritual depth. In the profundity of its utterances, the opening of St. John's Gospel brings the 'Good News' into full accord and alignment with the most exalted and ancient of all wisdom teachings, those concerning the Sun Logos.

It is here in the Prologue to this Gospel that St. John proclaims the Divine Word or the Solar Logos Being as having incarnated into a flesh and blood human body through Jesus Christ.

Of course, the mainstream Church was opposed to the cultivation of this vein of wisdom, especially in its complementary sophianic or feminine emphasis, because it worked so much against the centralist designs of the Roman theocracy which always managed to smell, in the great Johannine wisdom, traces of the despised pagans and their often anarchic love of Nature. Nevertheless, this suppressive urge has never totally stopped this esoteric wisdom from being cultivated, and undoubtedly John Scotus Erigena is one of the chief figures who managed to keep it from drying up altogether. He was fully aware of the triune God in the fullness of its sophianic, as well as its Logos, revelation. There was indeed never a greater champion of this trinitarianism, in his capacity to keep alive the power of the ancient wisdom within the body of the Church, than John Scotus Erigena.

Erigena thus holds a somewhat paradoxical position in the history of Christianity. On the one had he can be looked upon as the father of that movement which gave to the established Church its much needed philosophical underpinning, i.e. Scholasticism. On the other hand, he and his philosophy may be regarded as the vehicle through which the despised ancient wisdom was actually kept alive *to some degree*, albeit a rather reduced one. It is therefore not difficult to understand how it came about that he was eventually branded a heretic by the orthodox Church.

Apart from his written works, however (copies of which happily somehow managed to survive the flames of the heretic-hunters!), the course of Erigena's life itself is a very good indicator of just how deeply the resistance to the sophianic spirit runs within the soul of the Church.

ROME RULES . . . OR ELSE!

John Scotus Erigena[40] first came to prominence during a religious controversy, in the 9th century, regarding the so-called Augustinian doctrine of 'double predestination'. It was thus during Erigena's lifetime that this particularly dark piece of Augustine's thought was being actively promoted by the Catholic Church. The reasons for this, we can justifiably assume, were that the doctrine quite simply gave to the more repressive and aggressive elements, now very active within the Church, the power to literally preach hell to those who opposed this Church's authority. The doctrine, in other words, was a vehicle via which the ultimate power over the superstitious minds of the ordinary people could be fully enforced: the doctrine of damnation. In essence it stated that *inside* the Church you went to heaven, while *outside* of it you quite simply went to Hell; i.e. every individual was predestined to one end or the other (double predestination), the only possible hope of salvation being, of course, within the (Catholic!) Church.

Erigena opposed this dualist doctrine vehemently! He called it 'a most cruel and stupid madness', for he could clearly see that evil does not emanate from God, but from man himself; more to the point, he knew that all of man's sin had been forgiven through the miraculous power of the

Incarnation. Thus, if Hell existed at all, man did not go there because of God but because of the evil choice or activity of the man himself, and the Church most certainly did not exist as the agent of a divine and everlasting punishment. Quite the contrary: it existed as a divine power of *atonement* in the world, a harbour of fullest compassion, perpetual spiritual renewal, and forgiveness!

None of these types of free-spirited ideas, however, washed down well within the mainstream Church, anxious as the majority of its dignitaries were to increase their arsenal of weaponry by which their Church could impose its authority upon the unruly masses. Thus it was at the Synod of Valence in 855 that John Scotus Erigena was condemned for his writing and teaching. And like that of his equally if not more controversial forebear, Pelagius, in the 4th century, Erigena's sublime wisdom, so alien to the ears and hearts of the hard-headed dogmatists surrounding him, was pronounced to be nothing more than a mess of 'Scots porridge' (*pultes scottorum*).

Nevertheless Erigena, thankfully, despite all this vilification, had his patrons and admirers, one of whom was no less a personage than the powerful French King of the time, Charles I, more commonly known as Charles the Bald. Erigena had been invited by this enlightened and pragmatic King, long before his anathematization, to take up residence in his Court School (in 845), and there Erigena remained for many years, teaching, studying, writing, and lecturing, even long after his official condemnation.

The heresy-hunters, however, were, as always, never very far away, and it appears that soon after King Charles's death, Erigena had to seek refuge once more. This time he found it in England, under the patronage of the English king, Alfred the Great. It is said that Erigena became the Abbot of Malmesbury. In any event, the hatred continued to be stirred up against him, his professed and highly articulated freedom of spirit being his only sin. The erudite medieval historian, William of Malmesbury, gives us a sordid account of what this hatred led to in the end. He claims that Erigena was eventually stabbed to death by some of his so-called students with the nibs of their sharp pens! In this tragic fashion yet another brilliant light, heralding the free spirit of the ancient wisdom in all its wonderful incarnational renewal, was violently and cruelly snuffed out.

CHAPTER NINE

THE SPIRITUAL FLOWER OF CHRIST VERSUS THE 'DOGMA MACHINE'

————ooooOoooo————

John Scotus Erigena represents a vital link in the chain of survival of the esoteric knowledge of Christ and Christianity generally, a knowledge and a wisdom which has for a very long time been the focus of a concerted programme of suppression by the mainstream Church. The healing effects of this wisdom are very much needed again in our own day and it is very obvious that it struggles to re-emerge. For ours is a time of the very deepest longing in the hearts of ordinary folk for the ways of true virtue, for the keys to real meaning and wholesome values, in work, play, and in life generally. Esoteric Christianity has the potential to fill this vacuum because it draws upon the richest veins of wisdom the world has ever known but which have tragically been almost forgotten in our technological jungle. But now that the days of the heresies and the witch-hunts are hopefully over (in the Western democracies at any rate!), there is a real possibility that Esoteric Christianity could resurface.

However, such a revival can only come about if some clear understanding of the causes and the manner of this suppression are understood. It would be wise, therefore, to look a little more closely now at Erigena and his epoch in particular, for so formative was this period in terms of its influence on the development of European history that we are still very much involved with unravelling its ramifications. From the point of view of our particular study here, we have to say that this period of our recent history was one in which matters concerning the spirit were to play an overriding and vital part.

It is true that if one looks closely enough at any movement on the stage of world history there lies the individual human spirit itself. Regarding the development of the medieval culture in particular, however, one can discern how this spirit, in its deepest and truest relationship to Christ and the manner in which that relationship was defined, was *the* paramount question. Moreover, it was a question which also underlay virtually all of the period's exoteric, outer, or purely historical developments. It must be remembered that this was the Age of Faith, albeit a dark faith and one which, as we have seen, rested squarely upon a blind belief in dogma. But it is especially 9th century Europe that seems to us now a most strange, dark and confused period. Moreover, it was a time in which the Church strove hard to keep alive and promote this faith in the truth of the Incarnation, while at the same time knowing full well it had to be able to 'explain' it plausibly. This it undeniably did, with varying degrees of erudition and sincerity. However, the finest bequests from mankind's purely philosophical heritage, the arts of logic and reason, certainly did not constitute part of the Church's strength at this time, having from very early on in its institutionalized life cut itself off from true knowing or reason, i.e. from 'gnosis' *per se*, as we have seen. Rhetorically and dogmatically asserted articles of faith, doctrinal formulas, papal bulls, and carefully crafted ecclesiastical missives – all these and more represented the Church's growing points during these hard and difficult times. Logic and reason as such only began to have a real impact much later, when Scholasticism came into its own and especially when it reached maturity in the person of Thomas Aquinas (1226-1274).

But with the disappearance of the old Roman imperial order, and with it the quality and stability of life and manners that were part of this order (all of which by the 9th century were hardly more than a memory), and with the great mass movements of the tribes still unfinished in their repercussions, Europe was at this time a place ripe for an attempt at a form of government that would be both trans-national and in tune with the ordered discipline of the Roman Church. And in its body as well as its soul, Europe thirsted intensely for the arrival of such a secure state of affairs.

DIONYSIUS THE AREOPAGITE

The hierarchical system of government which was to emerge, feudalism, was one with which the Church could easily identify, as well as actively encourage. Under the astute influence of Charles the Bald, feudalism took hold in France and soon began to spread out from there.

Furthermore, at a time when both the Church and the State needed to find ways to bolster their respective positions from the point of view of a recognized spiritual or incarnational authority, it is not very surprising that they should look to great or heroic Church figures of the past for inspiration. In this way another figure soon begins to emerge in the unfolding tapestry of this medieval order. Though he is one who was long dead, his spiritual teachings nevertheless survived and were still cultivated to some degree, especially in the Eastern Church. Moreover, this individual was recognized as the traditional Apostle of France. We speak of St. Denis, who was the first Bishop of Paris and who subsequently suffered martyrdom for his faith at the hands of the Roman governor there. What is more pertinent to our investigation, however, is that this was the same Denis whom the Greeks identified as Dionysius the Areopagite. It will be remembered that Dionysius had become the personal pupil of St. Paul when he (Dionysius) converted to Christianity from the old pagan or Gnostic wisdom which he cultivated in the School of Athens (see Chapter 5).

We shall return in a moment to this 'French connection', but first a few general words about Denis or Dionysius, for his place in the history of Esoteric Christianity is crucial.

It is a fact that Dionysius eventually became (and remains!) a very controversial figure in the mainstream Church, something that is entirely bound up on the one hand with his direct link to the ancient Mystery wisdom, and on the other with the Church's active suppression of it. This suppression may be demonstrated historically in many ways, but from the standpoint of this focus on Dionysius it is most clearly illustrated by the fact that no sooner had Christianity itself been made into the state religion of the Roman Empire than the Emperor (Justinian) ordered the closure of this ancient School of Philosophy in Athens where Dionysius had studied and taught! The great tragedy of this act of utter ignorance, from the point of view of the general spiritual welfare of the nations, is that this was by then the only remaining place in the civilized world where people could still, after the defeat of The Gnosis, freely occupy themselves with the task of bringing the ancient star-wisdom of the human race into harmony with the great new incarnational religion of Christianity. But this was a work to which Rome was vehemently opposed from the beginning, as we have seen.

This closure by Justinian happened in the year 529, thus bringing to an end for a very long time to come all possible hope of a spiritual harmonization between the ancient wisdom and Christianity. Moreover, this was only the most blatant of a number of acts of suppression carried out by this Emperor in his misguided and grandiose plan to bring the newly confessed 'Christianity' of his empire fully into line with Rome's age-old patristic and militaristic origins, a regime which wanted nothing whatsoever to do with the ancient Temple wisdom. The irony is that this strange man proceeded with his egotistical plan, despite, or perhaps indeed because of, the fact that his empire was rapidly falling apart!

It is no coincidence, therefore, that around this same

time the work of Dionysius became the subject of a 'doctoring', the primary intention of which was to discredit as much as possible the ancient wisdom that inspired it. Notwithstanding the fact that this doctoring would fail in the end to achieve its goal (for the ancient wisdom is also, we must remember, the *perennial* wisdom), it has over the centuries resulted in a spiritual confusion unending in its capacity for provoking intellectual controversies.

Intellectual controversy aside, however, even in the diluted form in which the writings and teachings of Dionysius the Areopagite have come down to us, nothing is more obvious than that they appertain to a form of knowledge and a depth of wisdom which, though this constituted the very foundation of the early Church's teachings (from the 1st to the 4th centuries approximately), the modern Christian knows virtually nothing of them. This comes about because of the (hopefully short-lived) success of Justinian's efforts. He and others like him were successful because their opposition to, and suppression of, the true spirit has led to modern man's almost complete alienation from any kind of clear or sustaining relationship to the esoteric reality that underlies our sense-perceptible world.

Broadly speaking, modern man's knowledge of, or feeling for, the true spirit is only capable of expression when experienced, if at all, through a cloud of mysticism, of mystic or highly personal jargon, which more often than not does nothing more than make spiritual matters even more confused than they already are.

Any return to a full, true and clear understanding of the spiritual nature of man and the cosmos within the context of the incarnational body of the Sophia-Christ must on the one hand eschew any irrational mysticism and yet on the other hand be able to maintain the apostolic link with the Gospel of Christ and its obvious Mystery nature. The great significance of Dionysius the Areopagite is that he provides us with this link! This at least is something we can be quite clear about. Over the centuries this process of the elimination of the ancient wisdom from mainstream Christianity has progressed considerably, and the vital work of healing the psycho-spiritual split within the individual human soul which this suppression has inevitably caused, as well as the broader work of Church (spiritual) unification itself, is a huge task for mankind now and into the future. It must nevertheless be done!

DIONYSIUS DEFINES THE ANGELIC WORLD

Even way back in the 9th century, however, there was, one could say, an instinctive and acute alertness to the spiritual danger inherent in this process of Romanization. This was most keenly felt perhaps by the French more than any other nation on the Continent at the time. It was, after all, the Frankish tribes who, through their independence of spirit, constituted a prime factor in the eventual demise of the Roman Empire as an effective political unit. Charles the Bald, however, shrewdly alert to the deeper forces at work within his realm, as well as being fully in tune with the spiritual psychology of this time, showed his capacity to act in accordance with a wisdom higher than the merely conventional by sponsoring John Scotus Erigena to translate the work of Dionysius the Areopagite from the

Greek into Latin. This was in the year 858. Through this enlightened initiative, it became possible for the sophianic mystery spirit to at least maintain some sort of a presence within the conventional Western Church, however fugitive or controversial it may have had to become by dint of the forces of opposition upon which it continually came. Although the teaching and writings of Dionysius had been well known in the Greek-speaking Church and culture (i.e. in Byzantium), their injection into the by now dead letter of the Latin language at least gave the wisdom of the Areopagite an intellectual currency in the West which it would not otherwise have had. Indeed, it is nowadays quite well recognized by independent scholars that it was primarily the availability of these, more than any other writings, which constituted the core of whatever may be called spirituality in the Western Church from the time of their translation by Erigena onwards. Without them, it can be confidently argued, even the barest semblance of the mighty spirit of the Incarnation may have become totally and irretrievably lost.

What Erigena, through Dionysius, essentially did was to take the ancient temple wisdom of the Initiates, and the knowledge they cultivated from time immemorial of the powers and potentates residing in the heavenly bodies and the starry constellations (in other words, the gods), and translate it all into a context that would be in harmony with the fact of the Incarnation. Thus, the most important book of Dionysius, the one on the trinity of the spiritual hierarchies (The Celestial Hierarchy), gives Christian names, and what we may call an incarnational order, to all the gods of the ancient Mystery religions. In the language of Dionysius, the god Mars and his hosts came under the heading of Mights, those of Saturn under Thrones, those of the Moon under the Angels and so on. These correlations can be confidently made through a spiritually informed understanding of the work of Dionysius.

This, of course, constitutes the core reason why they have had such an aura of suspicion around them!

However, once we begin to orientate ourselves correctly regarding the supernatural or Mystery nature of the Incarnation and how in its most sublime expression in the Gospel of St. John this event is seen and described as the descent of the ancient Solar God, the Logos, into a human being, we can have little difficulty with Dionysius.

For then he emerges as our best available witness from the early Church in all these difficult matters, allowing us through his wisdom to focus on Christianity in its deepest essence, which is actually, when properly expressed, a continuation or culmination of the perennial wisdom. Moreover, his writings underline the fact that Christianity will only be fully understood when it is seen as a thoroughly modern renewal of the most ancient secrets of God, secrets the wisest men and women have always studied and striven to share with their followers.

One need not enter into the technical, astronomical, philological, or indeed any other of the disputations which revolve around the figure of Dionysius in order to appreciate the obviousness of this. One need only read, say, his letter (No. 7) to Polycarp[41] to realize how deeply imbued Dionysius was, and also how technically conversant he was with, the finer points of the ancient solar Mystery wisdom, a wisdom which he knew found its culmination in the powerful Event of the Incarnation. To take just one example, consider the solar impact of the Earthly death of the Sun God on the outward or physical heavenly body or bodies themselves. The Canonical Gospels merely say that at the time of the Crucifixion the Sun went dark. Dionysius, however, who was a witness to this astronomical event, in his letter to Polycarp describes its miraculous nature and does so in fascinating detail; moreover, in an effort to refute a disbeliever, who was nevertheless a very wise man (the Sophist Apollophanes), he places this marvel within the context of a much more elaborate and ancient solar astrology, or star wisdom.

****

Something of the working of benign Providence can certainly be seen, therefore, in the timing of the translation of these extraordinary writings of Dionysius for the Western world in the dark 9th century. Being instigated by a secular ruler, however, this work of translation by Erigena inevitably had for Charles the Bald an element of astute political practicality in it also. Charles could undoubtedly appreciate that the essentially hierarchical but purely divine wisdom of the Areopagite would accord well with the more down-to-earth temporal and ecclesiastical designs of the growing Church. He would also have had an eye to the fact that the writings would be capable of giving a sort of spiritual backup to the newly emerging structures of the (also hierarchical) medieval feudal order, an order he was moreover actively encouraging.

This hand-in-glove relationship of Church and State, a

situation which has a fine expression in the figure of Charles the Bald and which was the hallmark of the whole medieval culture, was entirely dependent on the notion of a terrestrial hierarchy (as the still current – though fast fading! – usage of the word 'hierarchy' to donate the Catholic Church's authority well illustrates). We may easily understand, therefore, that it was due principally to the fact that Dionysius could speak, out of his initiation wisdom, of a similar hierarchical structure in the spiritual world, and perhaps this alone, which prevented his writings from getting the decisive chop like so many other wisdom writings which various Christian sages produced over the centuries. It is evident that here, regarding Dionysius, the heretic-hunters were content merely to fiddle with his writings rather than burn them (which they could easily have done) for they are a veritable compendium of the ancient wisdom put into a purely Christological framework. Moreover, it is evident that they arise out of a true initiation knowledge (Dionysius refers explicitly to this), and were the products of a highly developed 'gnosis', all of which spelled anathema to orthodoxy from the 3rd century onwards. They should therefore have been high on the 'index' of the spiritual witch-hunters. However, like the original writings of Erigena himself, which also miraculously survived the thorough-going burnings by the skin of their teeth, for the wrong reasons, but nevertheless intact, these writings of the Areopagite have thankfully been preserved for us. As such, they stand as a valuable testimony to the spirit of Esoteric Christianity and point to a knowledge sublime beyond description. It is a testimony to the Christ as the spirit of a pure white magic, a magic which will not be extirpated however great the opposition to it may have been in the past or indeed may yet become in the future. Thanks to Dionysius (and others), in our very own time this wisdom has a greater possibility to blossom than it has had for many a long day. For though we live in a time of great religious confusion and moral uncertainty, it is also a time of great spiritual freedom. In former days, it was the Church itself which defined the parameters of this freedom for the individual. Nowadays, however, individuals themselves, especially if they live in one of the Western democracies, are relatively free to choose in matters of spirituality. This is so because we can live now (if we so choose!) without the death-sting of excommunication and so forth hanging like swords of Damocles above our heads (although it has to be said that remnants of such impotent and rusty legal weaponry still exist in the religious arsenals).

It is, however, out of a sense of the spiritual freedom tangible in our own time that a book such as this one you are now reading could actually be written at all. For even up until quite recently, the criticism levelled against the Church, especially the Catholic Church, which this book contains, would hardly have been permissible (especially in Ireland), or even if it was, it would undoubtedly have been met with great intolerance. For highlighting as the book does the very core of that which constitutes a true and genuine spirituality, as well as trying to trace historically the vicissitudes of this spirit, it depicts how the Church has largely been the agent of a spiritual repression rather than what it is meant to be, i.e. a conscientious upholder of the deepest power of the Incarnation.

CHAPTER TEN

A TRAGIC DENIAL

In our historical survey of the spirit of Esoteric Christianity we are passing the point of the 9th century. But before moving into the medieval period proper and then on into more recent and current times, we shall have to look at certain events towards the end of this 9th century which, though little is known about them by historians generally, are nevertheless hugely significant and revealing as far as the history of the West and especially of Western spirituality is concerned. Moreover, they are events which in a very real sense are an inevitable outcome of all that had gone before. The consistent drive, from the 4th century onwards, to suppress all direct knowledge of the logosophical spirit within the body of the Church led directly to those tragic events we will now examine.

The 9th century always puzzles historians. If the previous

centuries were dark, then the 9th may be best described quite simply as the darkest of all. Little can be said with certainty about it, but what we can say is that much was astir below the surface, deep in the soul of Europe at this time. The cultural blossoming which was to come somewhat later in the 11th and 12th centuries was surely brewing in the strange stew of the 9th.

We do know that the Church was, as it were, 'jockeying' at this time for the best possible position as the 'straight' of the Middle Ages began to unfold before its deliberating eyes. The manner in which it now begins to set the tone of its authority in readiness for this can be judged by certain crucial events which we will now describe.

The crux of the matter of the Middle Ages, as every historian knows, is to do fundamentally with the whole problem of *authority* as such, and its proper exercise. Where does it come from? And who is entitled to it in an *absolute* sense? Pope or Emperor? In other words, is it temporal or spiritual in origin? These were the key questions on the minds of most thinking people at this time. We have seen just how difficult such questions always were for the Church, especially since it could never truly get to grips with the deeply spiritual aspects involved because of its early and wanton abandonment of the Mystery wisdom.

THE HOLY SPIRIT IS DENIED BY THE CHURCH

By the 9th century, however, things had heated up to such a degree that the Church sorely wished to sort it out once and for all! It felt it simply had to, if it was to gain clear-cut power in the temporal world! Whatever else it was doing at this time it must not be seen to be dithering with regard to this most crucial question of spiritual authority. The Church, in other words, had reached a point where any talk of 'spirit' within the confines of its orthodox teachings had become little more than a cause of confusion, embarrassment, and conflict. Nobody seemed to have any idea of what spirit meant anymore. And so, in the latter half of the 9th century, this whole process reached its ultimate climax. It was in the year 869, at the Church Council of Constantinople, that a formal declaration actually *abolishing the spirit* was finally and shamefully made!

This tragic fact, however, was an almost inevitable outcome of the course the Church had taken from the time of the defeat of The Gnosis onwards. Quite simply the keys to a true knowledge of the spirit were by this time virtually lost! In a sense the only honest thing to do was to make a formal and binding declaration that there was in effect no such thing as spirit anyway. And this in effect is what one of the Canons of the Council of Constantinople[42] did when it declared to be heretical the Mystery teaching that the human soul is not one, but two, one part of which is entirely of a divine essence and therefore may be regarded as being *purely spiritual*, unlike the soul generally, which has a sentient aspect.

This is the precisely correct interpretation of this particular Canon from the point of view of the ancient wisdom, and an Initiate[43] of this wisdom is specifically referred to in the Canon and singled out for anathematization by dint of his teaching regarding the Trinitarian spiritual knowledge, a knowledge which knows, and has always known, that man consists of body, soul *and spirit*.

Before proceeding further, therefore, we will recap briefly as to how such a diabolical situation could have arisen in which a crucial declaration by a Church Council abolishing the spirit could not only have come about in the first place, but that such an abhorrent denial was felt to have been in need of a formal and dogmatic canonization. This recap is necessary in order that the fullest possible picture emerge as to how this incredible denial by the Church could have occurred. Following upon this recap we will give the precise details of this denial of the holy Sophia spirit.

****

Ever since the defeat of the Gnostic Church in which the ancient Mystery temple wisdom had mixed freely with the new incarnational wisdom, cultivation of knowledge of the spirit and the spiritual world was anathematized. What this amounted to was the complete abandonment of the very Mystery through which the Incarnation was made comprehensible, i.e. the light of Sophia. As we have earlier shown, at the heart of all the ancient wisdom lay the Trinitarian knowledge of man's relationship with God. One-third part of the Trinity was represented by Sophia or the Mother Goddess. She was rejected and the later leaders of the Church replaced her with the purely earthly mother of Jesus in a feeble effort to compensate for this most basic of errors regarding the sublime Mystery wisdom. It couldn't work! The Church was, by rejecting Sophia, also rejecting the crucial and precise focus of its origins, which lay within the sanctums of the Mystery temples and their initiation wisdom.

Sophia, as the Mother Goddess, had always represented the divine Wisdom. She was known and revered by the initiates from the time man first became aware of himself, his world, and his Creator. She represents the feminine or wisdom side of a divine wisdom/knowledge, feminine/masculine polarity. With the development of Greek philosophy, however, which began approximately in the 6th century B.C., this wisdom/knowledge, and with it knowledge of Sophia herself, began to emerge out from the secret 'holy of holies' of the temples and onto the wider stage of human affairs. Especially in the figure of Pythagoras (see Chapter 2) we see the Mystery wisdom being put forth in a manner now more suitable to man's evolving *self*-consciousness. (Prior to this, man's consciousness was far more tribal or ancestral. However, pure self-consciousness only fully emerged in the Middle Ages.) In other words, the whole vast edifice of the mono-theosophical wisdom (mono-theo-sophy = the wisdom of the One God) which had been cultivated and taught in the temples of initiation from the most ancient of days only to carefully selected individuals – this was all now being brought much more down to Earth and made accessible to individual human *thought*.

Individual human thinking-power, in other words, as opposed to the relative inflexibility of the gods' cosmic or nature-power, was now beginning to flex its own great and free spiritual muscle! Thus, what was formerly taught mainly through god-images, myths, symbols, and so on, now began to be put into the framework of purely human concepts and ideas. After the perceived revolution in the life of the human being brought about by the Incarnation, in which this whole free spiritual trend received a huge new

Sophia-inspired impulse, men inevitably began to debate hotly about the divine v human nature of the Christ. The whole direction of this Gnostic debate, however, worked very much against the sophianic or feminine manifestation of the incarnational spirit, a spirit which was moreover the very kernel of the Mystery knowledge but which found less and less a voice within the mainstream Church, eventually coming to constitute only a tiny part of it, in what might rightly be called the esoteric Church. So, in the East initially, and later also in the West, this true spiritual wisdom retained a fructifying presence, something which was due chiefly (though not entirely) to the teachings of Dionysius the Areopagite.

THE EASTERN CHURCH V ROME

It was Dionysius, however, who proved a most difficult nut to crack for the heretic-hunters! Especially during the reign of the Emperor Justinian, when the imperialistic mentality began to exert itself most strongly in the Church, great efforts were made to banish all the Mystery-knowledge from the 'See' of the Church. Significantly, however, it was around this same time that the teachings of Dionysius then appeared in written form. Up to then they, or at least the essential and deepest core of them, like all esoteric and wisdom teachings, had been transmitted mainly orally. Thus, while it probably proved impossible to suppress these teachings of Dionysius, representing as they did a core knowledge relating to the deepest truths of the Gospel, they were placed under suspicion on a variety of counts, and because of this they failed to gain universal, canonical, or authoritative recognition. This was not, however, before the Eastern Church tried to win this recognition for them as an antidote to the repressive or more worldly noises that were always emanating from the direction of Catholic Rome and its gradually developing claim to be the 'one true and universal Church'.

Thus, at the general Synod of the Church held in Nicaea in 787, the 2nd Canon explicitly declared that study of the Gospels should be amplified by the Dionysian teachings. This canonical declaration was made because certain enlightened influences emanating from the East knew very well that if these writings were not quickly made canonical the Church stood every chance of losing *all* contact with its rich spiritual Mystery source, and would simply dry up as a truly Christian/religious movement, no matter how theologically refined the dogmas it promulgated regarding Christ might be. Moreover, a subsequent Church assembly held in 867 in the East declared the previous 'Dionysian' one of 787 to the '7th Ecumenical Council,' *ecumenical* meaning that its decrees were binding on the whole or universal Church of Christ. Needless to say this Eastern display of authority did not go down very well with Rome! The result was that political intrigue heated up fiercely immediately after this significant event, with, among other things, the Byzantine Emperor (Michael) being murdered, and this probably with the Roman party's connivance. The new usurping and murdering Emperor who replaced him, Basil, soon became the Pope's puppet in the emerging struggle between East and West for supremacy in Christendom. Pope Hadrian, who had been thoroughly baulked in his ambition for his Roman Church by the action of the Eastern Synod of 867, could now decide freely on what to do next. True to the Roman spirit, he went for the jugular and decided on the most resolute and bellicose form of protest. He could afford to do so for he had in effect the new Emperor eating out of his hand! Thus he (the Pope) immediately convened a Synod in Rome (in 868) and the Canons of the 867 Council were thereby deemed to be null and void. To make the point most aggressively, the documents pertaining to these Eastern canons were all publicly burned! In this manner the scene was set for the crucial and highly controversial Council of Constantinople which took place in the following year, 869.

It can thus be seen that the whole push from the Western, or Roman side, was for the total abandonment of the ancient Mystery wisdom which they saw as a threat to their great plan for a single, worldwide Church dictated from Rome, and Rome alone. Rome did, and indeed was always doing its utmost to prevent this knowledge from gaining any kind of official sanction within the orthodox Church. It seems moreover that it reserved its most bellicose and resolute of actions for the prosecution of this more than any other of its causes. The freedom of will and of action which the cultivation of the ancient wisdom necessarily promoted, based as it was on *self*-knowledge, worked totally against all that Rome had ever stood for.

Thus the trinitarian nature of this wisdom, a wisdom which knew man in his self-reflected spiritual essence to be an image of the tripartite God, was, at the Council of 869, to be finally and formally abandoned, and man declared to be of a *dual* nature only, a being merely of body and soul, nothing more. This dualist nature of the Church's teaching has remained ever since, and to therefore regard Catholicism as a truly monotheistic religion anymore, something which it claims to be, is nowadays quite without a philosophical foundation. From 869 onwards any further talk of pure spirit as a fully distinct part of man's total constitution, as distinct, that is, in essence from the soul as the soul itself is from the body – this true spirit and divine knowledge of man was thenceforth to be considered heretical and those who 'pay any regard or obedience to the decrees of the author of this impiety, let him be anathema, and outcast from the faith and fellowship of Christianity'.[44]

This is the sorry spiritual state the Church had finally reached by the year 869. Significantly, this Council also spelled the beginning of the end of Christendom as a power for the brotherly unification of all the peoples of the world, a practical ideal which also represents the esoteric core of all true religion. The promotion of this ideal, so very much needed in our modern world, is thus intimately bound up with a revival of the Mystery wisdom within Christianity which has its roots in the East.

THE CHURCH DIVIDES INTO EAST AND WEST

From 869 onwards the East and West begin to go their own separate ways. A global axis of Christianity, which had been created to some degree in the first millennium, through the alignment of the ancient Eastern Mystery wisdom with the Western Gaelic or Celtic Church, now began to fall apart rapidly. The Roman-dominated Western consciousness subsequently became ever more worldly orientated in its 'spirituality', something which was an inevitability ever since it had set its face resolutely and 'Janus-like' against the divine spirit of God. As the universal Church itself became more and more entangled in 'spiritual politics', East and West finally broke up into two totally separate spiritual and cultural entities in the 11th century, 1054 being the date history books generally give for this Great Schism of the unified Church. What was formerly and ideally meant to be universal, now took on the highly ambiguous and fearful presence of a spectral, dark, and divided self-spirit in human consciousness.

And as far as Christianity was concerned, mainland Europe now became the principal theatre of the world's spiritual battles and wars.

Left to itself, without, as it were, the 'mothering' influence of the sophianic Eastern wisdom, the now fully despiritualized Western Church could 'carry on regardless' with its worldly ambitions, and this it surely did, and in an ever more militant way. In time its Scholastic philosophy would develop to such a degree that, especially through the enormous influence of Thomas Aquinas, one could justify doing almost anything in the name of Christ. Even the supremely unchristian travesty of all-out war was deemed to be acceptable in certain circumstances. The mighty and growing power of human thought, which the Scholastics developed to an extreme degree through Aristotelian logic, was now entirely on their side. Thus it mattered far less with what this thinking should concern itself than that it should 'prove' its point. Certainly from our perspective, this infatuation with Aristotelian logic can sometimes look more like the triumph of absurdity than anything else. (We are reminded here of the famous medieval dispute carried on with the greatest of earnestness and sincerity among theologians and philosophers as to precisely how many angels it was possible to balance on the point of a pin!!).

Thus, although the medieval mind was entirely engrossed in unravelling the meaning and purpose of the Incarnation, logical proof was in the end all that mattered to it. Thought itself therefore was the Church's latest and greatest addition to its arsenal of weaponry as the great European war-games, initially of words, progressed.

The outcome was that now anything became possible with thinking, so long as you logically made the basic division which was the linchpin of all Scholastic philosophy, i.e. the division between God and man, and asserted axiomatically that you could know nothing about God, the spirit, or the spiritual world. All this was stated to be entirely a matter of *faith*, the content of which was to be determined fully and exclusively by the Church's 'divine' teachings and must therefore have nothing whatever to do with ordinary human thought or feelings. It is interesting on this score to observe, therefore, how Thomas Aquinas was in due course given an almost divine status, becoming a sort of 'angelic doctor' whose bag of words contained all possible cures the Church could ever require. He duly spawned a whole new generation of Catholic theologians, and is capable even to this day of inspiring them. It has to be sated, however, that thought alone, or mere words as such, as far as the Mystery wisdom is concerned, is never final. Feelings must be allowed to enter the overall picture also, and this is part of the 'problem', if you like, of Thomism: its intellectual sharpness is gained at the expense of pure feeling. Herein lies a great danger, and until the implications of this danger are fully understood, it will remain.

A certain dualism is thus seen to emerge regarding the Christian religion. It was this very dualism which was the root cause of the intellectual pride and arrogance of the now totally de-spiritualized Western Church which was gaining ground in the Middle Ages.

'Give me the dogmas,' Thomas could boldly assert, 'and I'll supply the proofs!' And so in all of this we can observe how the 'Church Militant' was beginning to get into its full stride.

THE ISLAMIC THREAT

It will be clear to anyone who looks into these matters thoroughly that the eventual triumph of Thomism was entirely bound up with the defeat of something which the Church at this time perceived as a great threat. It can thus be said that the Church had in effect no choice but to sharpen up its act at this time. The threat that was now asserting itself was of a very fundamental, even archetypal order. It was called Islam.

On the one hand this was seen as a *temporal* threat insofar as Islam was an aggressive, militant, even militaristic movement encroaching into the territory of Christendom. On the other hand, however, it was also perceived as a *spiritual* threat insofar as behind Islam stood a highly sophisticated culture and philosophy informed and embellished by some of the finest minds the world has ever known.[45] The Church was right, therefore, to feel threatened in the face of this latest onslaught.

Thus it was that Arabism, or more specifically Islam, now took on the face of 'the enemy' for the Church! A great new heresy, perhaps the greatest ever, had arrived on its very doorstep, and with it a whole new negative focus entered the consciousness of Christendom.

With the spiritual wall between Eastern and Western Christianity becoming ever more impenetrable, however, and with both sides of the Christian divide increasingly going about their own separate business, the colour of heresy now had to take on a somewhat different shade. Thus it was that Rome came to find in 'the infidel' a powerful new target for its heresy-hunting, an activity which had become almost instinctual to it by this stage. The temporal advance of the Arab empire provided this focus on a basic level. On a higher or more spiritual level, however, in the Arab's denial of the divinity of Christ, Rome could hardly have found a better target. With this as its backdrop the stage was now set for a whole new phase in the overall development of the Christian movement in the world.

PART TWO

THE SECOND MILLENNIUM:
A LEGACY OF CONFLICT

CHAPTER ELEVEN

THE HOLY GRAIL AND ESOTERIC CHRISTIANITY

Many subsequent events in the history of Europe illustrate very well the sort of sclerosis the Church underwent after it had finally and formally separated itself from all knowledge of the spirit in 869. We shall look at some of these events in detail a little later.

Now, however, we will attempt to show the general way in which the sophianic spirit managed to survive in the Church at all, albeit and necessarily in an ever more concealed manner. In illustrating this phase of the history of the esoteric spirit of Christianity we shall, therefore, have to consider most carefully something which, ever since it made its first appearance in the literature of the West, has proven to be an endless source of mystery and speculation as well as scholarly investigation.

Its route into the folk consciousness of the West is not an easy one to unravel, but it certainly owes a lot to Arabism and orientalism generally in that it is an object of the greatest magical and mystic significance. The whole idea of magic is, of course, in the Western consciousness at any rate, very much bound up with the mysterious Orient.

What we speak of is also a vessel symbolic of this ancient Oriental wisdom in its deepest and purest sense. This is the Holy Grail.

We shall now examine this question in some detail. But before doing so we should first say a few words about how the Incarnation comes to be so intimately connected with the Holy Grail.

The reader will undoubtedly have noticed how we have placed the Event of the Incarnation at the very centre of our discussion of the history of Esoteric Christianity. We have moreover assumed on behalf of the reader a certain amount of very common knowledge regarding the Incarnation. It should be said here, however, that the overall nature of our study precludes any theologically nuanced discussion, for we are only too well aware how theological argument can, for the general reader, often serve more than anything else to dull the spiritual importance of the Incarnation! Such discussions may, of course, be fine for the intellectually minded. This book, however, was not written for the intellectually minded only, but for everyone possessed of a healthy sense for the questing nature of the human spirit, as indicated in the dedication at the beginning. One need not be an intellectual to have questions regarding the true meaning of life! Likewise, neither must one be an intellectual to answer them!

Thus it may be said that what is most important of all regarding the Incarnation for people generally is that it is food not just for the spirit alone, but for the body and soul as well. Health of the body is intimately related to health of the soul, and insofar as Christ can be regarded as the archetypal Healer of man, any proper contemplation of his Incarnation must take the archetypal Christian meal, the Last Supper, fully into account. For it was here that Christ magically poured his entire Being into the Chalice. The Chalice then became the unique Christian symbol of the soul's nourishment, that by which the soul would in time be fully healed, even to the point of overcoming death itself. It is for this and similar reasons that the Holy Grail found a place in the soul of Western man. It encompasses in an holistic way the full reality and overwhelming importance of the *healing* power of the Incarnation. That is to say, it appeals not just to our sense of logic, reason, or our historical sense alone, but to the imagination also, and thus to our whole subconscious life out of which our will impulses are born.

Such thoughts raise many questions regarding the Grail. It is, however, the very answering of these questions that represents what has always been called the Grail Quest. This *quest*-ioning may indeed be regarded as the very lifeblood of the legend of the Holy Grail. Imagination is paramount to it, and any who take up the Quest diligently will find that it is a Quest full of magic and mystery, just like our dreams. It is entirely to do with the healing power of the imagination.

Unlike the Incarnation itself, however, we must speak of the Holy Grail in terms of legend rather than history. For if nothing else, logic demands that when we talk of the Incarnation we mean (among other things) the *actual*, the real deification of the flesh (the 'word made flesh' of the Gospel). The Incarnation *by definition*, therefore, cannot be regarded as a legend.

The fact that the Holy Grail has come to embody so much of what we may term 'incarnational lore and legend' has a lot to do with the fact that the mainstream Church has not been able to accommodate, within the boundaries of its narrow, theological, and dogmatic framework, the Mystery and mythic element which the Incarnation justifiably engenders in the soul-life of man. The mainstream Church cannot do this since it denies to the Incarnation the essential Mystery continuum around which all such poetic, imaginative, and even subconscious activity would naturally coalesce. This is just another reason why the Holy Grail has proved to be such a fascinating object for so long, especially among poets and sensitives alike who, by their very nature, will always be the first to suffer the ill-effects of spiritual repression. To the poets we owe our real knowledge of the Holy Grail.

THE HOLY GRAIL – FACT v FANCY

A substantial library could be filled with books about the Holy Grail. Many of them, however, are spurious, like a lot of esoteric literature. One can get happily (or indeed very unhappily!) lost groping around in the murkiness which an undisciplined approach to this fascinating, albeit often confusing, subject can engender.

We will not, hopefully, add to the confusion during the

few pages we will now allot to this subject, which is, however, despite all the irrelevancies, fundamental and very central to the study in hand. Indeed, one can go so far as to say that in the Holy Grail we have the very symbol of Esoteric Christianity, and that is why Esoteric Christianity may also be called Grail Christianity. As we shall presently show, the Grail can be most easily and instructively seen, from a purely spiritual point of view, as that object which best signifies the transition from the ancient and esoteric temple Mysteries to the new incarnational Mystery of Christ himself. The Holy Grail did not achieve any such recognition in the mainstream Church precisely because of this Mystery connection. Quite the contrary! Due primarily to the Church's repression in this regard, the consequence was that the Holy Grail became that object around which coalesced, in an imaginative way, all the disparate threads of the extant ancient wisdom which were by now well scattered upon the winds by the Church's relentless hostility. The Grail thus became the individual soul's focus through which the 'oversoul' of Europe could continue to legitimately cultivate the sophianic Mystery wisdom, and do so in an imaginative and deeply meaningful way.

Traces of the ancient Mystery wisdom continued to exist in many of the magical but, by the Middle Ages, largely superstitious practices of the folk cultures. In this milieu, however, during the Dark and Middle Ages, the Holy Grail became an object which had the effect and intention of Christianising this Mystery or magical element. In this dynamic lay its appeal, its efficacy, and its rise as a symbol in the consciousness of Western man.

Although the Grail legend is woven from many different

threads including pre-Christian and pagan ones, in the West it came to be identified pre-eminently with the Cup of the Last Supper. This was the same Cup in which Joseph of Arimathea was said to have caught some of Christ's blood and which he (Joseph) subsequently brought to England.

During the centuries of the Church's sustained stamping out of the ancient wisdom, the Grail symbol gradually arose within the Western folk consciousness as representing that great depth of Eastern, or of oriental wisdom generally, which had culminated in the Incarnation. It filtered into the Western consciousness in many ways, not the least of which was through the now fully established and thriving Islamic culture. During the otherwise Dark Ages, Islam had become a great force for the enlightened pursuit of knowledge and wisdom in many places within its realms, but most importantly, perhaps, for Europe, in Spain. Here, apart from more orthodox pursuits, Islamic mysticism, magic, and the whole hermetic and temple wisdom generally had taken root very strongly. Islam itself did not see anything particularly special in the Event of the Incarnation, did not indeed admit even to its occurrence. Islam had, however, risen to prominence partly because it had been able to pick up on those aspects of the Mystery wisdom which the Church had jettisoned in its dogmatic drive to 'spell out' the uniqueness of the Incarnation. As a result, Arab culture became one in which a rich magic played a vital, fructifying, and central part.

THE POETIC IMAGINATION AND
SPIRITUAL REALITY

Stories about magic cups and cauldrons were quite familiar within the oral folk culture generally, but as the Christian culture of the West gradually developed, with its poets no doubt looking longingly beyond the Pyrenees and towards the Islamic and Oriental world generally and the magic being worked there, the stories about the Holy Grail seemed to them the best possible way of transmitting their inspiration regarding their Christian conception of the spirit and the spiritual world. (The question of the validity of the spirit or the spiritual world was not a problem for these poets, just as it is never a problem for true poets anywhere. This is something which, like the saints themselves, they never have very much need or reason to doubt.)

In this way the Grail stories eventually came to be written down and thus put into those literary forms through which our exoteric knowledge of the Holy Grail has been transmitted. This did not happen until much later, however – the end of the 12th century and the beginning of the 13th century, to be precise. In fact, virtually the entire corpus of the original Grail literature was composed within a short span of 50 years or so. All the rest of what we know exoterically about the Grail stems from these works and all other and subsequent artistic and poetic work worthy of the name is based on them. From the point of view of our present study, this in itself is quite significant for it implies almost a 'rush into print' before it was too late! For very soon afterwards, the great upsurge of Grail Christianity known as the Cathar movement was to be annihilated by the Church with a frenzy, hatred, and fanatical violence that have never quite been equalled.

We shall come back to this catastrophe in the next chapter, but here it should be noted that the Grail stories reached the highest point of their development in the work of the great medieval German poet, Wolfram von Eschenbach, who in his extraordinary epic poem, *Parzival*, raised the Quest for the Holy Grail to a level of high art.

Eschenbach indeed is said to have been a member of the aforementioned Cathar movement. In any event, he tells us categorically in his poem that his knowledge of the Grail was transmitted to him through a Spanish wizard called Flegetanis.

THE STONE FROM HEAVEN

Although Wolfram von Eschenbach does not speak about the Grail explicitly as the Chalice of the Last Supper, the manner in which he does refer to the Grail implies his deep knowledge of it as that object by which the great Mystery wisdom of the Orient is connected intimately with Christianity. Eschenbach calls the Grail the *lapsit exellis*, an appellation which has puzzled scholars ever since it appeared, for it has several meanings. Apart from the obvious fact that it is the poet's prerogative to be manifold in his meaning and use of words, it is commonly agreed that *lapsit exellis* means the 'stone that fell from heaven' or something very similar. In the New Testament, Christ on a number of occasions is referred to in 'petrific' terms (e.g. 1 Peter 2:4: 'So come to him, our living Stone'). This is the obvious sense in which Eschenbach means the 'heavenly stone', especially when it is coupled with the Oriental legend wherein it is related how a jewel from God's crown once fell from heaven to Earth and was thereby fashioned by angels into a precious cup.[46]

The cup as an image or symbol which signifies the passing of the ancient Mystery temple-wisdom of the East, through Judaeo/Christian influences eventually to the West, is best illustrated by recalling an incident in the Old Testament where it is pretty obvious that what is being spoken about is precisely this great and very important transitional moment in the spiritual history of the world. The Old Testament does this by presenting to the reader a figure straight out of another world. He appears from out of a background of which we know little, but of which we nevertheless can sense great depths: the Mystery temple-culture stretching way back to the ancient oriental world and beyond.

This is the figure of Melchizedek who can perhaps lay claim to be *the* most mysterious of all the early Old Testament personalities. The twilit nature of his appearance, however, is lit up once we become aware of the fact that he actually represents a vital link between the ancient, secret, temple-wisdom of the very remotest antiquity, stemming from the Orient, and the newly emerging and more outgoing form of this wisdom which the gathering nation of the Israelites represented. In the Book of Genesis Melchizedek appears, as it were 'out of the blue', as an extremely exalted figure, and confers on the greatest Patriarch of the Jewish nation, Abraham, a blessing in the name of the 'God Most High'. This, together with other references to Melchizedek in the New Testament *Letter to the Hebrews*, clearly indicate that Melchizedek was a highly exalted initiate of the Mystery temple-wisdom, one of those individuals who almost invariably, as we have already seen, worshipped the One God, i.e. was monotheistic in his religion.

The writer of this *Letter to the Hebrews*, it must be remembered, would most likely have been privy to much oral, esoteric, and Cabbalistic knowledge in this regard. Thus he can speak to the Hebrews in a very authoritative and revealing fashion about Melchizedek, saying that he is a representative of 'their first principles of the oracles of God', and that he enters 'through the veil'. The veil in Jewish thought and in the temple rituals represented that which divided the mundane or secular world from the divine or spiritual world, the 'Holy of Holies'. Melchizedek is thus seen to confer upon Abraham an initiation into the most ancient of the wisdom-teachings stemming from the mysterious and farthest depths of the Orient. These were the same monotheistic and perennial wisdom-teachings that were going to become, in time, the very bedrock upon which Moses would eventually forge the Hebrew tribes into a cohesive nation, for they represented an initiation ultimately into a knowledge of the Creator. Melchizedek is for this reason also likened in the *Letter to the Hebrews* to Christ himself, who now performs, the writer tells us, the same kind of initiation to all who turn to him, and does so moreover in a direct line of succession from the ancient temple wisdom, but in a manner that is nevertheless totally new and free from the yolk of the Law.[47]

What is even more to the point, however, in relation to our consideration here of the Holy Grail specifically is that Melchizedek bestows his initiation on Abraham by giving him bread and wine (Genesis 14:18), an act of the deepest symbolic significance. What the bread and wine emphasizes most clearly is the continuity between the very ancient Mystery wisdom, the Judaic Mysteries, and on into the new Mystery of Christ. It indicates, in other words, the direct link between the central ritual sacrifice of the temple Mysteries of which Melchizedek was a representative, the subsequent Passover Meal of the Hebrews, and on into the later Mass of the Christians. Thus, the central ritual of the very first Christians, that 'agape' gathering which was later to evolve into the Mass, has its origin in the ancient temple Mystery-rites of initiation. This is very clearly indicated by the figure of Melchizedek.

THE LAST SUPPER

Christ is also referred to as the Lamb of God many times in the New Testament, the Lamb in this case representing more the purely Hebrew Mysteries, for at the Passover meal the Pascal Lamb was always eaten. However, at the Last Supper (which was the last ritual meal of the old covenantal order as well as the first one of the new spiritual Mystery of Christ), the fulfilment of the Jewish blood-rites is achieved and a return to a purer and more spiritual form now becomes possible and is hereby inaugurated. Thus it is over the *vegetarian* species of bread and wine that Christ utters the ultimate words of the incarnational miracle. From that point onwards the Cup, as the Holy Grail, becomes the host of the new sophianic and incarnational Mystery Deed of Christ, was well as being the absolute symbol for his continued presence in the world.

Herein lies the real meaning of the Holy Grail, for in the lives, minds, and imaginations of those Christians most intuitively alert to the true spiritual nature and origin of man, a knowledge which was nevertheless being systematically stamped out, the Holy Grail in the Middle Ages became the vessel into which was poured from many different sources the now Christianised modes of this perennial/esoteric wisdom. It is with this in mind that we must appraise Eschenbach's hero Parzival, who, as the Grail winner, has been justly called the blueprint or archetypal forerunner of the fully enlightened Christian personality.

The Quest for the Holy Grail can be pursued in many ways. To place too much emphasis on its claim to reality as a purely physical object in this search is, however, to miss the point, just as it would be to place too much emphasis on the purely historical side of the Incarnation itself, at the expense of the Mystery aspect. Like all other pursuits in life, balance here is the key to success, and meditation is the key to a balanced life.

We therefore offer the reader the following Grail thought as a thanksgiving meditation:

In memory of the Last Supper, the first Christians celebrated the 'agape' or 'love-feast'. This ritual differed from preceding Mystery rites in that it was no longer a human or an animal that was being sacrificed, but a God. By partaking in this Christ sacrifice, human blood is purged of its animal nature and godhood is offered to the human being.

This meditation, calling attention to the essential holiness of food, can strengthen and solidify one's faith in, and love of, the Christ, like no other.

CHAPTER TWELVE

THE ALBIGENSIAN HOLOCAUST

———ooooOoooo———

The rise of the ecclesiastical Roman power in the West, which fed itself with a negative power through its growing and intense hatred of the occult and everything and everyone connected with it, was determined to stamp out all traces of true spirituality. This very hatred, however, was accompanied, as we have seen, by a concomitant rise of the Grail legend in the folk consciousness, i.e. the consciousness of the ordinary people. This development took place throughout the Dark and early Middle Ages. It represented, one could say, a sort of soul fermentation, coalescing imaginatively around the sophianic and Mystery spirit of the Incarnation. The pagan and magical elements which clung to these folk cultures, despite all the antagonism directed against them by the Roman Church, actually survived in many ways *because* they found a focus in the

Holy Grail. The Church was highly suspicious of this because it smacked of nothing but 'paganism'. The Grail or Chalice thus very significantly never achieved any status or recognition within the official Church, unlike many other of Christ's 'relics'. To give credence to any kind of Grail or esoteric spirituality, in other words, would have meant risking supporting something which went totally against the grain of Rome's authority. What the Church was most determined about was that there should be no challenge to its supreme authority as the guardian and sole director of the religious and spiritual life of Europe. However, the institutional Church, having become by the 12th century a major political power (coupled with the inevitable ill-effects resulting from its complete rejection of the spirit earlier) had fallen into utter decadence. Many of its dignitaries and clerics were now openly living totally profligate and immoral lives.

In southern France, this overall situation added momentum to a religious movement which although it was Christian in essence, was nevertheless evolving in a manner that was totally independent of Rome, just as the Celtic Church had similarly done many centuries previously. Moreover, it was a movement which, although it cultivated an unorthodox form of Christianity, was nevertheless far nearer in spirit to the roots or origins of Christianity than was now the case with the conventional Church.

The movement we speak of is the Albigensian or Cathar movement, which spread rapidly in Europe during the 12th century.

We shall now look fairly closely at this movement, for by doing so we will be able all the more easily to appreciate the fact that ever since the abandonment of the sophianic Mystery spirit by the conventional Church, this spirit had nevertheless continued to, as it were, bubble beneath the surface in all manner of ways. And we shall see that it was this undercurrent of psychic and spiritual activity in the soul of Europe which came to a head in the historical Cathar movement.[48] Furthermore by the time the conventional Church really began to take notice of it, the Cathar movement had evolved into an elaborate and fully fledged mystery/spiritual organism. It was a sort of spontaneous expression of a spirit which had for far too long been forced into an underground existence, but which eventually surfaced here in 12th century southern France into the full view of history as an organized and deeply religious movement. Thus we can say that the Cathar movement was a bona fide expression of the Mystery spirit within the parameters of Christendom itself.

THE HOLY INQUISITION

In order to illustrate this, however, we will not be able to satisfy the demands of academic orthodoxy. For it is a fact that most of what we know regarding these medieval Christians comes from the records of the Inquisition which, it is very important to keep in mind, was initially set up to eliminate them![51] Thus, relying solely upon the records of the Inquisition for information regarding the Cathars, would bare the same relationship to relying only on Nazi records to get reliable information about the Jews!

One thing that we can say for certain is that the Cathar movement was hugely significant, one way or another, in the eyes of the Church, given that it had to resort to such vile methods as the Inquisition to deal with it. The result is that much misinformation is passed on about the Cathars, especially in encyclopaedias etc., where they are mostly dismissed simply as 'heretics'. Here, however, we will appraise them in accordance with the point of view of Esoteric Christianity. We know that they taught reincarnation. In the West, this doctrine had long been denied to the masses, even before the advent of Christianity. Virtually nothing of it is taught exoterically in Judaism, either, although it is hinted at, as it is in the Christian scriptures also.[49]

THE CATHARS AND THE ANCIENT WISDOM

Because of the lack of reliable information about the Cathars, scholars are usually puzzled about their amazing growth, especially in southern France in the 12th century. Where did they come from? Who originated their ideas, beliefs, and practices, etc.? Merely labelling them as 'gnostic' or 'heretics', as is usually done, does not get to the root of the matter. However, when one views them in the light of all that had gone on previously within the Church with regard to its suppression of the spirit and of true spiritual knowledge, the Cathar movement may be better understood. From this point of view one of the most revealing and significant things about them is that they are generally believed to have been in possession of some fabulous treasure. Leaving aside the fact that to be in possession of deep spiritual insight is to possess treasure, it is not difficult to see that even if they had lots of gold, silver, and jewels, to have the 'keys to the Kingdom' could be easily mixed up, by greedy-minded materialistic people, with mere gold or money.

Significantly, the treasure of the Cathars was rumoured to be the Holy Grail itself! This is significant because it suggests that the Cathars were teaching the inner path to Christ, which is the Grail path. We can confidently assert that what most antagonized the Roman Church was that the Cathars were teaching a direct spiritual or individual experience of God. The word 'Cathar' itself implies this, for the initiation experience is a kind of 'catharsis'. This and other aspects of their teaching earned them the 'gnostic' label. This 'gnostic link' was also the primary reason why such terrible hatred was stirred up against them, a hatred which led eventually to nothing less than an all-out war against them by the Catholic Church. It was an atrocious genocidal war which, by the time it ended had left a whole people slaughtered and a vast area of southern France, the Languedoc, blood-soaked and totally devastated. This is the conveniently forgotten war of European history and is known generally as the Albigensian Crusade.

THE CATHARS: THE PURE AND PERFECT ONES

There were other reasons, of course, why the Catholic Church undertook this, perhaps the most demonic of all its acts of repression so far. The fact was that the Cathars, who by the very nature of their movement did not need a hierarchical or centralist structure, were nevertheless by the time of the Crusade coalescing into a clearly defined Mystery-wisdom or esoteric movement within the Church's jurisdiction. Though they did not have priests as such, they did have a structure whereby degrees of initiation were available to members. Thus, if one became a convert one could eventually progress from being an ordinary outer member to an inner one by becoming what they called a *parfait*.

This word actually means a 'perfected one' and incorporates some of the deepest aspects of the esoteric or perennial wisdom, Christianised: the Way of Perfection. The *parfaits* could be either men or women. The ceremony or ritual in which this confirmation took place was known as the *Consolamentum*.

The Cathars were, by the beginning of the 13th century, at a stage of their development whereby they were organized territorially into areas of jurisdiction, something akin to the diocese of the Catholic Church. By then they even had bishops (or the Cathar equivalent). By this time also, although their greatest stronghold was the Languedoc province of southern France, they were gaining a following in various other parts of Europe, most significantly in urban centres of Germany, Flanders and Champagne.

Needless to say, no matter what their beliefs or practices were, all these developments were hugely threatening to both the temporal ambitions as well as the spiritual authority of the 'one true Church' (in Rome!). Indeed, by now the Cathars were beginning to look as if they were openly challenging the orthodox Church's authority, and moreover seemed even to have the potential to become a sort of rival 'catholic' Church in Europe, all of which was anathema to Rome. Indeed, how could they be regarded by Rome as anything other than heretical? Inevitably, therefore, the dreaded demon 'heretic' was once more pulled out of the Roman closet, this time dressed up in suitably despicable apparel and given the label 'Cathar'. This monster was duly deployed in *the* most terrifying of ways yet conceived for him. These Cathars had to be taught a lesson, and the most effective way the 'Church Militant' had of teaching now was the way of brute and terrible force. And by God did they start to use it!

THE DEVASTATION OF THE LANGUEDOC

The culture which arose in the Languedoc in southern France in the 12th century is said by historians to have been the most sophisticated and advanced that Europe had yet achieved, something which was due in no small measure to the presence of the Cathars. They were also harbingers of the deepest tenets of the ancient Mystery wisdom which had always, from time immemorial, been the wellspring of the very best aspects of culture and civilization. The Languedoc had thus acquired a wealth and a luxury that was, by the 12th century, the envy of many of its neighbours, but especially the northern nobility. The Church unashamedly exploited this greed and envy for its own purposes, and when one of its Papal Legates to the Languedoc was murdered (not, as it turned out, by the Cathars) on 14 January 1208, the Church found just the excuse it needed to set in motion one of the bloodiest episodes of its long history. Immediately after this Pope Innocent III ordered a Crusade against the Cathars, offering all kinds of enticements to those who joined, like the cancellation of debts to Jews and the remission of all sins past *and* future, not to mention of course the rich booty to be had, and so on. Needless to say, the Pope soon amassed a huge rabble of an army.

Not long afterwards, this rag-bag of an army set out marching, and on 22 July 1209 they entered the town of Beziers, one of the Cathar strongholds. In an evil orgy of violence, the entire population of this town was massacred. It is estimated that 30,000 innocent men, women, and children were slaughtered on that unimaginably terrible day!

This event set the tone and marked the opening of an awful war against these innocent people which lasted for about 20 years, at the end of which the vast area of the Languedoc lay devastated, its culture and its deeply religious people utterly annihilated. It is impossible to calculate how many died in the course of this conveniently forgotten war.

The extermination of the Cathars and their movement was obviously meant to be total! Not the faintest trace of them was to be left on the face of the Earth! And in this the Church more or less succeeded. Of course, it is not possible for history to completely whitewash the horror of events such as this. Something of them eventually comes to light in the general consciousness. As we piece together more knowledge of the Cathars and their movement, it will surely be seen that here we have yet another example of the perversion of Christian truth, the massacre of innocence and goodness for the sake of political expediency, and the triumph of narrow and dogmatic intransigence over what is perhaps the most necessary of all Christian virtues: religious tolerance.

CHAPTER THIRTEEN

THE DANGEROUS SECRET OF THE KNIGHTS TEMPLAR

While the Cathars represented an esoteric movement which grew up outside the strict parameters of the medieval Church, there were nevertheless also within the orthodox body of the Church many signs that this spirit was still active. In passing we may mention a movement like the Fraticelli, also known simply as the 'Spirituals'. Another was the Brethren of the Free Spirit. There were many others.

However, the most successful, widely known, and significant but nevertheless also the most tragic of all these esoteric spiritual movements was the Knights Templar.

One may say that the spirit of Esoteric Christianity came to a sort of climactic expression in the Church in this great movement, which was inaugurated very early in the 12th century. (The year 1118 is the most widely accepted date for the formation of the Knights Templar.)

The Templars is a movement which has always intrigued historians, not least because of the aura of mystery, legend, and rumour which surrounded them during their lifetime, a mystique moreover which continues to this very day! Like the Cathars, the Knights Templar seem to have had about them a certain indefinable 'something', a 'something' which has its roots in their essentially esoteric nature. It is a 'something', however, which will always remain not much more than that unless or until the overall triune framework for recognizing the reality of the sophianic Mystery spirit is adopted by historians.

However, before developing these points further, let us briefly consider some of the outer and more important historical facts regarding the Templars. In doing so, let us try to keep in mind something of the atmosphere of the high medieval culture which gave birth to this, perhaps *the* most fascinating of all movements which Christianity has begot in its long, 2000-year history.

We have referred previously to the hierarchical nature of medieval society, and also to its highly structured and loyalty-based feudal system of government. But perhaps the most conspicuous of all aspects of this medieval world, and one which is intrinsically bound up with hierarchism, was the way in which it was almost totally immersed in the Gospel story. Hardly any part of the medieval world was left untouched by the Incarnation, and virtually all learning and cultural activity centred upon it. Thus, at this time of the high Middle Ages, in a very real sense the Church was universal. The general period is, for this reason, known as the Age of Faith. We must also remember that the

Incarnation was unambiguously taught by the orthodox Church to be a fully *historical* reality and that mythology and the like had nothing to do with it. Here ironically lay one of the greatest strengths of the Church's teaching. For this reason, also, the faraway and mysterious Holy Land, where the Incarnation drama was known to have actually occurred, was regarded as a place of huge spiritual, religious, and symbolic significance in the consciousness of medieval man.

Symbolism played into the make-up of this medieval consciousness in an all-pervasive way. In virtually every aspect of his outer life, as well as deep within the feeling life of his soul, medieval man was (as even the most cursory acquaintance with his world will show) highly absorbed in, and preoccupied with, ritual, gesture, and their symbolic significance. His consciousness differed very much from ours in many ways. He or she was for instance far more imaginative and inward in his or her soul-life, compared to our highly abstract and extroverted mode of consciousness. In consequence, his or her religious life had more to do with feeling than with pure, conscious, or abstract thought. Most people cultivated simple virtue far more than any kind of deep spiritual knowledge. Notwithstanding this, however, those who did pursue knowledge could deepen their soul and spiritual life all the more easily if they so wished, and do so moreover in a way that is most difficult for us nowadays, for we have largely lost touch with this feeling aspect of the spiritual life.

MEDIEVAL MAN AND THE IDEAL OF PIETY

For medieval man, therefore, his religion played into every aspect of his life, his thought, and especially his feeling. In this way Christianity grew as a great social force in the Middle Ages, out of a powerful, yet simple and virtuous faith in Christ Jesus.

Most particularly for medieval man it was in the matter of *fealty*, a virtue which provided the moral basis for the entire feudal system of government, that manner and custom was carefully regulated in his society. Symbol and symbolic gesture thus had far more power, spiritual and otherwise, than they have nowadays. In this milieu, we can easily understand the religious passion and fervour with which the holy places were held by the people in general.

It weighed particularly heavy on the minds and hearts of all deep-thinking men and women at this time in Europe that the Holy Land and all its sacred relics and highly symbolic shrines were in the hands of those who did not have the same feeling of fealty for, or anything like the same kind of belief in, Christ, as they did themselves. By the end of the 11th century, all of the Holy Land had been conquered from the Christian Byzantine empire by those most powerful of all heretics that had yet emerged to challenge Christianity, the Muslims (or more precisely in this case, the Seljuk Turks). And it was out of these deepest and most pious sentiments of the Christian Europeans that that other most notable feature of the medieval world then emerged, i.e. the Crusades.

Of course, there were many other factors besides this playing into this extraordinary epoch of the Crusades, factors as much to do with economics, politics, and so on, than directly with religion. But of the depths of piety, and of the genuine, though often blind faith practised by these, our medieval forebears, no one can have any doubt at all. Undoubtedly the High Middle Ages was marked more than anything else by a love of and a fidelity to Christ that was beyond the questioning of most. The kind of questioning that is so natural to our modern way of thinking, only came later. For the moment, however, it was the virtue of piety which most fructified the spiritual soul of Europe, and it was by dint of these very same sweet-longing and pious sentiments that medieval man could only behold in those who did not share similar feelings, nothing but pure *infidelity* towards Christ! In this manner the concept of the hated 'infidel' arose and was duly woven into the complex texture of medieval European thought.

It would not be far off the mark to say that the Knights Templar represented the very cream of this kind of pious medieval man. Just prior to their formation, the Holy Land had been recaptured from the hated infidel in the first Crusade. Very soon a few of these most highly motivated and pious men, obviously delighted by this great victory, got together and decided to create an organization dedicated to the protection of the holy places and their pilgrims. This was ostensibly the original purpose for the formation of the Templars. The manner in which they went about this formation indicates very clearly that the deepest of thought and the most careful preparation, both spiritual and temporal, went into it, to ensure that their Order would be comprised of the very best types of men in society.

It is obvious when one looks into the origins of the

Knights Templar that from the very start they were intended to be primarily an elitist organization, but elitist in the best sense of the term. Elitism or hierarchism was, after all, the very dynamic of medieval society. The Templars were thus meant to be an institution that was in strict accord with the prevailing mentality. Totally unlike the Cathars whose movement was in essence a spontaneous grassroots expression of the deepest spiritual fervour of the times, the Templars from the beginning intended to harness this fervour into the most disciplined kind of order and the most carefully prepared and thought-out organization imaginable. Though historically they are recorded to have begun in the year 1118, it is obvious from a close study of the facts that this is merely the date on which they, as it were, 'came out'. Many years of preparatory work had gone into the creation of their Order, whereby a network of approvals, blessings, and fealties from the very highest in society had been obtained before they went public.

It should be noted here that this was also the time when the mendicant Orders were coming into play as a vital force. This is quite a separate story, of course, but the Templars in a sense may be seen as taking as their ideal a sort of marriage of two of the most notable features of the medieval Christian world, Friarhood and Knighthood.

THE TEMPLARS AND THE GRAIL CASTLE

The original group of Templars who gave birth to these ideals was actually very small, less than ten. But something of the depth of the purely esoteric wisdom which inspired them can be gauged from the fact that the Order was not long in existence when one of the most influential and wealthiest Counts in all of Europe at the time, the Count of Champagne, joined them. The significance of this may be understood when it is realized that it was at this Count's court in Troyes that there had long been flourishing a Cabbalistic School of esoteric wisdom. It was there also that the Grail romances received their first airing. This happened chiefly through the poet Chretien de Troyes. Indeed, the Grail connection generally is very strong with the Templars as it had also been with the Cathars, indicating clearly that here, in the heart of Europe, the deepest aspects of the ancient sophianic Mystery wisdom of the East was being cultivated. Wolfram von Eschenbach, the author of the greatest of the Grail romances, *Parzival*, is also known to have visited the Templars in Palestine, and in his epic poem he accords to them the unique and high distinction of the guardianship of the Grail. All this points directly to the arcane nature of the Templar's motivation and the deep esoteric inspiration behind the foundation of their movement.[50]

Moreover, in Eschenbach's romance, which is actually full of arcane references, the Grail Castle can easily be understood as referring symbolically to that world beyond the threshold of the physical senses, a world of which those who engage in depth meditation become aware. Indeed, the whole of the romance of *Parzival* may be regarded as an attempt by Eschenbach to give this mysterious though often chaotically perceived spiritual, astral, or etheric world an ordered frame or point of reference based on the Christian Mystery. In this we may also come to understand why he gave to the Templars the guardianship of the Grail

Castle,[52] for he would have been aware of their great reverence for this mysterious world behind the everyday one, an understanding of which they would have gained through prayer, meditation, symbolism, and ritual.

We have already clearly demonstrated in previous chapters how the whole thrust of the Church had been, from very early on in its history, focussed on a denial of this spiritual wisdom, and actively suppressed the cultivation of it. It was precisely because of this that the Catholic Church had then no choice but to base its structures of theocratic authority on only a partial image of man. As we now know they deemed man to be essentially devoid of spirit, saw him as a body and soul only, a terrible blunder. Strictly speaking, therefore, the Church had become something of a headless beast, for it denied the very thing from which it should, by the nature of its assumed authority, have gained its greatest strength.

The soul-sensitive and truly enlightened ones in the Church's midst, however (always very few in number!), saw through this woeful anomaly. And by virtue of their cultivated wisdom and knowledge they acquired a genuine and deep spiritual authority which the mainstream Church possessed, as an institution, only in a skin-deep form. It was these very same sorts of men who were the backbone of the Templar movement, thus creating an institutionalized and genuine spiritual authority in a Church which did not have it in any real sense.

This is the fundamental reason that these men were feared and respected throughout the length and breadth of Christendom during their all-too-short history. And feared and respected they surely were! For only one man, the Pope, was ever above them in authority, and he never crossed them.

THE TRINITY OF VIRTUE: POVERTY, CHASTITY, AND OBEDIENCE

The Templars were deeply pious monks. They took the already well-established Christian institution of Knighthood and turned into an inspired and highly disciplined religious Order dedicated to fighting for the Christ. Because it arose within the parameters of the orthodox Church, and also because of the careful preparations laid before it became fully public, once it did, it rose very rapidly in power and influence. Though never great in numbers, it attracted into its ranks the most idealistic and pious Christ-inspired men of the time. Many of these were very wealthy, and as a consequence the Order soon became very wealthy itself. For when a man joined, he put all of his resources, however vast they were, into the hands of the Order. No individual knight was ever allowed to own anything himself, for all were, as true monks, subject to a vow of poverty (as well as chastity and obedience).

At the zenith of their power these pious horsemen were the bankers of Europe. They were even put in charge of Royal treasuries.

It was only to be expected, however, that as the Order grew in strength, privilege, and prestige, individuals of a lesser moral calibre than that of the original founders joined. And undoubtedly, like in any large institution, there were some who abused their authority. All this, coupled with the inevitable envy they stirred up in kings and nobles who resented their power, authority, and especially their secrecy, eventually created something of a backlash against them. And greedy, envious eyes began to be turned upon them and their wealth.

THE GREEDY KING

It was in such an atmosphere that malicious rumours about them were spread abroad and began to grow. Towards the end of the 13th century (by which time the Muslims had regained entire control of the Holy Land once more, thus in a sense vitiating the Templars' reason for existing), the time was ripe for an attack against them by their enemies. This, when it came, was spearheaded by one of medieval Christendom's most vicious and greedy monarchs, Philip IV of France. It was this cold and cruel king (also known ironically as Philip the Fair), who, having systematically squandered his people's resources, had left himself and his country in a state of near bankruptcy. Then with his eyes firmly set upon the Templars' vast wealth he exploited the rumours circulating about them, concocted spurious charges against them and laid a meticulous plan to outlaw their organization and thereby gain for himself their great wealth.

It was a plan worthy, in its conception and precision of execution, of, say, a modern military dictator's harshest crack-down on his strongest opponents. For precisely at dawn on Friday 13 October 1307, all the Templars in France were arrested and their property confiscated in one quick, sharp, and highly organized round-up.

Soon afterwards the full force of the Inquisition was brought down upon them. The rumours about their strange, ritualistic activities and the attendant images of devilry and debauchery that the spirit-fearing and spirit-denying Church built up out of these rumours were now collated into a body of so-called evidence against them. Much of this was gained through confessions extracted under the severest forms of torture.

There is one feature of the Templar's confessions, however, which has received perhaps more publicity than any other, and that was that they confessed in many cases to secretly worshipping a god who bore the name of Baphomet.

Baphomet was a dark mystery to the Inquisitors. He seemed an entirely original creation of the secretive Templars who would say little about him. Because of this also the records have bequeathed to us little more than the name. This god has therefore kept historians and scholars guessing ever since. However, a relatively recent piece of scholarly detective work gives us a good clue regarding the meaning and mystery of the Templars' Baphomet.

Dr Hugh Schonfield, who has written a number of interesting books on the origins of Christianity, published in 1956 one called *The Secrets of the Dead Sea Scrolls*. In this Dr Schonfield recounts his significant discovery of a cryptographic code which he found had been used to conceal from unworthy eyes the true meaning of certain esoteric names in early Gnostic or esoteric writings. He called this code the Atbash Cipher. It was a system of coding which, he found, was used in various texts, including some of the Dead Sea Scrolls.

In another book, however, published in 1984 (*The Essene Odyssey*), he turned his attention to the Templars, and specifically to their worship of Baphomet. By applying the cryptographic principles of the Atbash Cipher to this enigmatic name, he found that it decoded perfectly into the word Sophia!

Now, given what we have so far recounted in our book here, this is not actually very surprising. Indeed, one can justly say it fits the overall picture perfectly. For it was this Sophia Mystery wisdom which was most severely anathematized by the established Church, and hence the Templars had no choice but to keep it secret.

The fact indeed that we now know that Sophia lay at the very centre of the Templar's movement is perhaps *the* most revealing statement that we can make about them in respect of their being a movement which tried to bring to light and life, within the highly restrictive atmosphere of the mainstream Church, the perennial or Mystery wisdom. Herein lay their great secret and the source of their power. They were also, nevertheless, it has to be said, too far ahead of their time in trying to bring to light at that particular stage of history the Mystery of Sophia in Europe. They were indeed in many ways attempting the virtually impossible, given the Church's dogmatic and militaristic stance on anything to do with real spiritual insight. And for their efforts, the Templars suffered the almost inevitable consequences!

In France, the Templars were mercilessly put down, very many being burned as well as suffering imprisonment and torture. Because of the activities of Philip the Fair, who pressurized other monarchs in Europe into suppressing the

Templars, in many other countries also they were harassed and imprisoned. Indeed, Philip's hatred of them seems to have had no bounds. Significantly, it was also only under pressure from Philip that the Pope himself, who in any case had always been Philip's puppet,[53] agreed to officially dissolve the Order. This happened in 1312. And this, it should be noted, was done without ever an official pronouncement of guilt being made against them by the Church, something which undoubtedly indicates a deep respect, if not indeed a great fear of them, which lingered to the bitter end.

The final act in this spectacular and tragic spiritual drama of the Middle Ages came in March 1314 when the Grand Master of the Order, Jacques de Molay, and one of his chief colleagues were slowly roasted to death in an horrific *auto-da-fe.*

Just before he died however, Jacques de Molay apparently made two very significant statements. One was that his confession, which the Inquisitors had extracted under torture, was totally untrue. The other was that he called his two principal accusers, King Philip and Pope Clement, to join him before the Throne of God within one year, to answer for their actions. And both of these men were actually dead within a year of de Molay's execution!

Although the Templars were officially disbanded in 1312, they continued nevertheless to exert influence in one way or another for many centuries afterwards. In Scotland, for instance, they were never officially dissolved at all. In other places, they joined the ranks of similar types of organizations like the Hospitallers, organizations which they themselves (the Templars) had been the inspiration for in the first place. But Christendom was never to see anything even vaguely like the Templars ever again.

Nowadays, however, as we travel around Europe we are constantly reminded of them and also of just how widespread their power and influence was during their brief history. Virtually everywhere we come across 'temple' in a place name (one indeed is never very far from such a place), and we can be fairly certain that there the Templars had exercised their power, influence, and great authority in the service of Christ, pursuing rigorously the very highest of Christian ideals in the pure light of the great logosophical Mystery wisdom of the Incarnation.

CHAPTER FOURTEEN

THE SPIRIT OF THE ROSE CROSS

The defeat of the Templar movement marks the final attempt of the spirit of Esoteric Christianity to find a true expression within the confines of the orthodox Church. From here on, the cleavage between the Church and this spirit becomes ever more pronounced.

At this point also we begin our entry into the modern era with all its attendant complexities regarding the soul and spiritual nature of man and his relationship to the world. Here in the 14th century the stage is being set, as it were, for the later triumph of materialism at the shocking expense of the spirit, a trend which has in a certain sense reached its apotheosis in our own time, the beginning of the third millennium.

Up to this point we have been observing how, apart from its very early wonderful flowering in Palestine immediately after the Incarnation, the esoteric spirit of Christianity was gradually eschewed by the body of the Church. This, we have seen, occurred because the Roman-led Church placed virtually all its emphasis on building up the purely temporal body at the expense of the much more significant Mystical Body. This Mystical Body, to which the Church normally paid (and may even still pay) only sterile lip-service, represents the enduring and true reality of the Mystery of the Incarnation. Indeed, it can be said that if this esoteric aspect is not cultivated, developed, and proclaimed in a manner at least as diligently as the outer or exoteric one, the 'body' will quite simply die!

This Pauline analogy between the body and the Church is very apposite and instructive here with regard the great tension that has developed between the inner and outer aspects of Christianity. Just as the physical human body will soon die of thirst for lack of clean, pure water, so too will the temporal body of the Church die if it continues to be denied the 'living water' of the esoteric spirit. It is in this manner that we must come to understand what is meant by the Mystical Body. Through this way of thinking we may come to truly appraise the current crisis in Christianity.

THE RISE OF THE SECRET SOCIETY

This split condition of the Church, which was chronic from the early centuries, only became acute in the High Middle Ages. Exoterically it led eventually to the great cleavage we know as the Reformation. Esoterically, however, this cleavage gave rise to a phenomenon which has remained with us in some shape or form ever since. What we speak of here is the phenomenon of the 'secret society', something which, though it features in all epochs of history, proliferated in the Middle Ages.

Depending on the reasons for their existence and the methods they deploy to achieve their goals, such secret groups can gather unto themselves great, though subtle power. In an epoch as ordered and controlled as the Middle Ages, they undoubtedly had far more power than they would in our own much more open world.

Given what had happened to the Cathars, the Templars, and others, it was inevitable now in the 14th century that if Esoteric Christianity was to be cultivated in any organized way at all, it had to be done in total secrecy. By now it was overwhelmingly obvious that the Church would go to any lengths to deny the secret riches of esotericism into mainstream Christianity.

Perhaps the best known (to us!) of these secret societies, wherein the ancient wisdom continued to be cultivated within the overall framework of western Christendom, are the Rosicrucians and the Freemasons. It is very hard to estimate the extent of the influence these Brotherhoods had upon the social and religious fabric of the world in which they operated. Undoubtedly, however, such influence was very significant, especially during the time in which such societies were being most true to the spirit of the ancient wisdom.[54]

Nowadays much speculative literature is written about these and other secret societies, which by their very nature, we must remember, came into existence in order not only to cultivate but also to conceal as far as possible from hate-filled eyes the true nature of the Mystery wisdom. Such a paradoxical situation was inevitable, for as the history of the Church by this time had overwhelmingly shown, there were far too many people around who were hell-bent on destroying this precious jewel of the ancient wisdom, especially in its incarnational or re-incarnational aspect. It had therefore to be cultivated and promoted in the most subtle of ways imaginable, ways which to the average mind nowadays are almost impenetrable due to the sheer density of their symbolism. It is because of this that scholarship in this area usually does little more than unearth mysterious puzzle after mysterious puzzle, presenting the researcher and his or her readers with a sort of Pandora's Box of occult symbolism and allusion, astonishingly rich in content certainly, but also all too often devoid of any reasonable interpretation.

Any approach to these types of societies, however, which is not based on a positive acceptance of the validity and veracity of the ancient wisdom, as well as on a clear understanding that there was always afoot an active movement to suppress it, will do little more than add extra speculation to the already far too dense mystification!

What we will do here, therefore, and in order hopefully to avoid any further smoking of the mirrors, is to record merely the salient or most pertinent features (from the point of view of our present study) of *one* of these societies, namely the Rosicrucians. By doing so, we will be both able to illustrate, as well as get a feeling for, the overall place and significance of these kinds of societies within the ongoing development of the spirit of Esoteric Christianity in western Christendom.

THE WISE AND HOLY MEN OF GOD

Those who went by the name Rosicrucians were the ones who most securely and deeply bore within them the spirit of the ancient wisdom during this critical period of our Western history. By gaining some understanding of them, however cursory it may have to be here, we will, as it were, get a flavour of how the sophianic spirit, now a totally underground movement, began to work invisibly within the soul and culture of Europe.

The Rosicrucian Brotherhood was established in 1459 through the work of the Initiate known as Christian Rosenkreutz, who had made contact with the dispersed representatives of the now moribund stream of the Templar wisdom (among others). What Christian Rosenkreutz did was to give this dying steam of wisdom a great new impetus, for in the teaching and the character of this personality, the ancient wisdom came to a rich and modern maturity. He brought to it a new unity as well as giving it an updated and thoroughly Christianised expression, and was moreover able to organize and inspire the Brotherhood into a powerful esoteric movement.

Conventional historians, however, have difficulties with the apparent 'invisibility' of the Rosicrucians. Although they are well recognized as having actually existed and what they stood for is also well known, precisely who they were remains a mystery. We must say something about this here in an attempt to clear up the confusion.

In one sense the Rosicrucians, if they were going to work at all in the material world, simply had to work invisibly, given the history of the esoteric spirit up to this time. The terrible repression and persecution of previous individuals and movements which attempted to bring this wisdom to the forefront of the Christian consciousness were in themselves reasons enough for the Rosicrucians' apparent and cultivated invisibility.

There is, however, another reason, equally if not more pertinent than this. The fact is that the Rosicrucians were not so much concerned with the outer world of nitty gritty politics and so on as with the overall transformation of human thinking and consciousness along purely spiritual lines. Although they were highly active in all kinds of good social work, they saw their primary mission as an antidote to what they astutely observed as the purely materialistic trends in the society of their own time. Thus, as the foundation of their movement, they promoted, more than anything else, the creative and curative powers of the imagination. They were therefore in this sense a utopian movement primarily, and as such did not occupy any particular 'place'[55] on Earth but rather had their true place in the spirit or the spiritual world. In an archetypal sense this may also be regarded as the world of a purely *divine imagination*,[56] which by definition cannot be seen with physical eyes and could only be found through accepting and practising the Rosicrucians' own initiatory disciplines. Historians, needless to say, don't usually understand this! Hence to them the apparent invisibility of the Rosicrucians!

The initiation procedures of the Rosicrucian Order are illustrated or summed up very well in the name of their founder. The name Christian Rosenkreutz actually means the Rose Cross of Christ. This Rose Cross was the profound symbol of the Rosicrucian order.

It is a measure of just how little is generally understood by conventional or academic writers on the subject of the Rosicrucians that this symbol, itself undoubtedly the key to any esoteric or even exoteric understanding of the Rosicrucians, is usually misconstrued. It is for instance usually referred to as a cross which is rose-coloured, something which does not convey the import of its true meaning.

The Rosicrucians were a network of Brothers who went quietly through the world effecting good works of Christian loving service, and did so out of a great depth of knowledge and inspiration which they acquired through a spiritual training based principally on a profound meditation on the Mystery of the Incarnation. For them this was summed up in the symbol given to them by their founder, the symbol of the Rose Cross. This symbol is best represented, however, not simply as a rose-coloured cross but much more powerfully as a black cross with a wreath of seven red roses entwined around the intersection of the crossbars.

In this form, this symbol is probably one of the most profound of all Christian symbols and is indeed capable of unlocking infinite depths of spiritual wisdom in meditation. It sums up the Christian Mystery in a wonderfully pure and simple way. It also, however, in a very graphic manner throws much light on the fundamental cleavage we have been discussing heretofore, in that it defines the essential difference between the esoteric and the exoteric streams of Christianity, the latter's symbol being of course the Crucifix.

THE ROSE CROSS: SYMBOL OF
SPIRITUAL REBIRTH

Expressed at its most basic level the symbol of the Rose Cross indicates the following: the black cross is representative of the lower or earthly man while the roses are symbolic of the fact that out of this dark nature, the higher or spiritual Christ-man grows, through a process of purification of his blood. In this way the Rose Cross depicts the full Christian incarnational cycle of earthly birth, death, and eventual spiritual rebirth. Moreover, it also overcomes the severe limitations of the exoteric Crucifix, which concentrates on the death aspect only and as such has had a huge influence on the formation of the Christian psyche, an influence which has been by no means always benign.

Throughout the 16th century the Brothers of the Rose Cross were deeply inspired by their symbol and were consequently highly empowered spiritually, psychically, as well as physically in their work. They were for the most part very ordinary people, a network of tiny scattered bands, small in number but large in spirit, for they were Christ-imbued. They worked in all manner of ways and in an exceedingly quiet and secretive fashion. They had to! They had no choice! In this way, however, through their activities they kept alive in the undercurrent of European culture a stream of the pure spiritual 'living water'. This they managed to do in total opposition and in great contrast to the ever-growing forces of militaristically backed materialism, forces with which the orthodox Church invariably acquiesced.

It is important to remember also that by this time that

great upsurge and refinement of culture and learning, the Renaissance, had impacted greatly on the folk-soul of Europe. Fundamental and far-reaching changes were taking place everywhere at this time but especially in consciousness itself. Europe was now emerging out of the faith-imbued strictures of the Middle Ages and into the modern period of scientific enlightenment. That other great revolution was also in full swing, the Reformation. The invention of the printing press around this time also needs to be carefully noted, for this invention was mammoth in its implications. (This is an example of one of those rare events in the history of mankind, where all attempts at characterising its repercussions fail. One can merely draw parallels: the invention of the computer in our own day is of similar import and significance for man's development.)

Perhaps not quite as complex as our own time, 16th century Europe was nevertheless getting to grips with great new possibilities and ever widening horizons, both intellectual and territorial. From this time, all learning and culture, in fact consciousness itself, was taking on an entirely new dimension and a great new sense of individual freedom was arising.

THE DANGERS OF SHARING THE SECRET

It was the printing press especially that gave the word 'secret' a totally new dimension, too! For in an age when some piece of information or knowledge could be printed and disseminated by the thousands, what indeed could be really secret anymore? A situation had arisen whereby what formerly had been passed by word of mouth or by carefully copied and guarded manuscripts could now be replicated and circulated *ad infinitum*. It was in just such a milieu that the Rosicrucians moved from being a secret society to one publicly known to be concerned with the deepest questions of the day.

Thus it was in the years 1614 and 1615 respectively that the two famous Rosicrucian Manifestos appeared in the form of printed and widely circulated copies in Germany. In these documents a plea was made, on behalf of all those who were deeply influenced by the Christ Mystery and the ancient wisdom generally, for 'the establishment' to take up this wisdom and knowledge in a scientifically applied and consciously responsible manner, with the aim of a wholehearted and truly spiritual renewal of culture generally. In the following year, 1616, a third document, the mysterious *Chymical Wedding of Christian Rosenkreutz*, was published. This document went very much further than the others in that it gave in an imaginative narrative,[57] an account of the processes which occur in the human soul as it undergoes the various degrees of initiation into knowledge of the spiritual worlds of which the material world is, in terms of the ancient wisdom, but a transient reflection.

All of these publications managed to create a huge stir in the public life of Middle Europe at the time. Whether or not they had the primary intention of doing so, they certainly had the effect of both publicizing and politicizing the erstwhile highly secretive work of the Rosicrucians. When the excitement thus engendered was blended into the general air of intellectual and cultural freedom of the time, all this managed to raise widespread hopes for a spiritual regeneration of mankind, too.

For this was all happening at a time in which the Roman Church was becoming increasingly recognized as nothing but an obstacle to all such spiritual progress. However, the tragic downside to all of this, as far as the Rosicrucians were concerned, was that now that they had come to the notice of the establishment through the widespread dissemination of knowledge about them, their days were numbered. They were no longer 'secret' any more. Ironically now, it was this secretive aspect of their activities which was the author of their downfall, for it was this very secrecy which caused the taps of rumour and vilification to be turned fully on regarding them, and the frenzy of the heresy hunters once more was whipped into full swing. And so it was not very long after the publication of the Manifestos that the whole movement was, like many other esoteric movements before it, mercilessly crushed.

THE BOHEMIANS' LOVE OF WISDOM

The epicentre of the 'Rosicrucian Enlightenment' was the ancient and historic Kingdom of Bohemia, a place of the richest cultural heritage in Europe, which had, in the period preceding the time in question, also gradually become a place of the deepest Christian esoteric studies and of hermetic learning generally. Inevitably, therefore, it was here also that the Catholic forces of reaction gathered a fierce momentum against the Rosicrucians and their movement. Beginning with the defeat of the Bohemians at The Battle of the White Mountain on 8th November 1620, these reactionary forces, led here by the Duke of Bavaria, came down with a mighty vengeance upon this Kingdom.

From this defeat onwards, the Bohemians were subjected to the most frightful tyranny and persecution.

It was in this manner that what has come to be known as the Rosicrucian Enlightenment was very quickly snuffed out and yet another chapter in the history of Esoteric Christianity came to a tragic end.

Before this happened, however, the movement did manage to achieve something quite significant regarding the cultural/spiritual life, especially of Middle Europe, for it brought to a far greater awareness than would otherwise perhaps have been the case, the significant part that esotericism must play in any genuine spiritual or cultural renewal in society. The Rosicrucians came near to achieving such a renewal in Bohemia, and if they had not stirred up the heretic and witch-hunters would undoubtedly have spawned a much more general revival of arcane learning in Europe.

Like many other movements before it, however, the Rosicrucians, once their secrecy had been exposed, were considered to be a threat to the established religion and its orthodoxy of theocratic control. As such, they quickly became easy targets for the witch-hunters and were put down. Moreover, the events which followed immediately upon this elimination were such that any similar kind of esoteric enlightenment would never be allowed to return again. Very significantly, it was at precisely the same time as the Rosicrucians' defeat that another terrible catastrophe was unleashed in Europe by similar spirit-fearing powers. This time, however, the scale of the destruction was to be even greater, in fact very much greater, than anything that had gone before. It was a catastrophe which wrought immense cruelty and suffering upon people all over the continent of Europe. It is known generally as the Thirty Years' War.

Stated at its most basic level, the Thirty Years' War was a reaction against the progressive movement of the Reformation. What the Reformation had essentially done was to polarize into a stark clarity the already long-existing division within the Western Church, or more precisely, within the soul of Europe itself. The foundation for this division had been laid, was we have seen, way back in the very early centuries of the Church when the sophianic wisdom had been so tragically abandoned. This in turn led to the incredible denial of the spirit by the Church!

THE DEVIL APPEARS!

The Reformation was essentially an exoteric expression of this esoterically based problem, and though it achieved for the Church some advances, it has, from a larger perspective, done little more than highlight the crying need in Christianity for the purifying and unifying forces of the perennial wisdom. Only within the framework of the sophianic wisdom's tripartite concept of Man as a microcosmic reflection of the macrocosmic reality of the divine Trinity can a sure basis be found for a true healing of all the growing divisions in the psychological, spiritual, and religious life of modern man. This tripartite wisdom has, alas, been almost entirely lost.

The need for such a return to basics was sensed, if not actually consciously recognized, by the religious reformers of the 15th and 16th century. Inherent in such a return to basics, as far as the Mystery of Christ is concerned, was a breaking free from all law-ridden authoritarianism, and allowing the individual the freedom to find his or her own unique way into the truth of the Christ. It was, after all, this very freedom which in the first place had allowed Christianity to emerge out of the almost overwhelming legalistic restrictions of Judaism and enter into the wider world as a powerfully liberating, spiritual force.

After centuries of endless repression, however, the situation became critical in the 16th century and resulted in the splitting of the Western Church. Put into very broad terms, this splitting of the Church, on foot of the Reformation, was essentially an outward expression of an inward and deeply felt desire by the individual Christian to assert his true Christian right to know God through the spiritual power of Christ and Christ alone. The Roman Catholic Church was now beginning to be perceived as that entity which was actually preventing this. It therefore took on the guise of 'the enemy' from the reformer's point of view.

When once it became apparent, from the 16th century onwards, that an individual could pursue knowledge without regard for the Church's monopoly, or even worse, do so even without its approval, and yet somehow claim such pursuits to be Christian – it was this fact more than any other that caused the Church to, as it were, really shake in its boots and eventually crack in half. Simultaneously, something very interesting and very revealing happened. When all this 'unsanctioned' scientific investigation was seen to be threatening the stability and authority of the Church, these pursuits were denounced as devilry, for the extremely limited vision of the reactionaries caused them to see it in no other way! And so, significantly, around this time we find an archetypal figure emerging into the European consciousness, a figure who, although he is highly cultured and learned, is also nevertheless branded as being nothing less than a child of the Devil! This is the sinister, dark, but nevertheless alluring figure of Faust. (He got such a poor reputation because he was believed to have literally sold his soul to the Devil.)

Faust represents nothing less than the individualized expression (in an archetypal image) of all the turmoil that is being engendered in the European soul at this time and of which the Reformation is merely the outward or historical symptom. This emergence is very significant in that Faust, though a highly learned man, is also a very sinister one. On the one hand, he possesses all the finest embellishments and accoutrements that a civilized and cultured life of the Middle Ages could afford. On the other hand, it is clear that what we are now dealing with is yet another reinvention of the oldest of all the skeletons in the Roman cupboard: the heretic.

CHAPTER FIFTEEN

FROM HERETIC TO DEVIL

The birth of Faust in the soul of Europe at the time of the Reformation was an inevitability. Faust is indicative of a deep disturbance on two complimentary levels: the individual psyche on the one hand and the folk-soul on the other. What Faust does is to give an individual, artistic or imaginative countenance to a much more generalized or social problem of which the Reformation was merely the outward or historic manifestation. Thus, in trying to understand Faust or the reason for his emergence, we shall at the same time be getting to grips with the conflict between the esoteric and the exoteric which lies at the heart of the true spiritual quest.

These problems, though in Faust given a medieval setting, are nevertheless still with us today. They are, in other words, still totally relevant and, as such, account for the enduring popularity of the Faust theme.

Ever since the early days of the Church when it first took up its evangelical mission to the world, Faust had in a way been germinating or gestating in the imagination of Western man. He takes his initial conception from one Simon Magus, who makes a brief but very significant appearance in the New Testament (see Acts 8:9-24). This Simon Magus was a magician of very great renown throughout Palestine. He had recently turned to the new Christian Way, but was not yet, at the time the recorded incident takes place, fully initiated. (This point is specifically referred to in the Acts.) He comes to the attention of the writer of the Acts primarily because he tries to *buy* spiritual power from Christ's disciples. For this lack of insight, however, he is severely rebuked by the apostle Peter.

This incident may be viewed on a number of levels and is one which begs the whole difficult question of authority or power as such insofar as this plays into the ever-present tension between the temporal and the spiritual. It can be stated with confidence that this polarity represented one of the key tensions in the whole development of Christianity since its inception. However, as the centuries passed and the Church got further and further away from this episode, and from all the other historical events which surrounded the Incarnation, it also lost its ability to discern, in a truly spiritual manner, much of the subtle meaning in the Gospel. This situation was very much further compounded by the Church's active repression of the ancient wisdom. Dogmatic literalism then began to replace true spiritual discernment as the primary tool in evangelism, and so the written scriptural records in this manner gradually and inevitably became the bedrock of the Church's dogmatically enforced authority. The Church was now at liberty to interpret the Gospel, one can say, in whatever way it wished, in order to serve its own narrow focus. Thus, this particular incident regarding Simon Magus in time became the *ex cathedra* basis for judgement upon the practice of magic and the cultivation of esotericism generally. Moreover, this was always a judgement which, as we have seen, was universal in its condemnation and invariably cruel in its enforcement.

It was, and is, however, also a judgement which totally misses the mark if one reads the incident in the Acts carefully enough.

A close reading reveals that it is not Simon's magical powers (or even for that matter the very practice of magic itself) that is being condemned here, but something quite different. Simon, it appears, despite his newly professed Christianity, had a total misunderstanding of the Christian use of money, or more precisely of gold. Gold had a very special place in the consciousness of the early Christians. As the Sun metal, gold always had, for the practitioner of the ancient wisdom, the deepest of magical and alchemical significance. Because of this special relationship to the Sun and also because Christ was regarded as the Sun God or the Solar Logos in the early Church, how one used this precious substance from now on, especially among the new congregations, was of the very essence of one's worth or measure as a Christian.

CAN YOU BUY THE HOLY SPIRIT?

What the incident involving Simon is attempting to underline is that a new relationship to gold is now needed if one is to find one's way to the Christ Being. One must be prepared, even (horror of horrors!), to give it all away! There are other parts of the Gospel which stress this point also, but essentially the incident regarding Simon more than anything else points up the fact that the Christ-Spirit, when one truly has it, gives or should give one total freedom in the world, i.e. freedom in and from the merely temporal world, of which the 'money' aspect of gold is the most potent symbol. It was this very important part of the initiation that had not obviously tweaked with Simon! He brazenly or ignorantly tried to buy spiritual power with gold or money, and in this manner Simon Magus became responsible for a new kind of sin, and even gave his name to it: simony.

The early Christians, especially those who were fully initiated, placed the greatest of emphasis on a correct understanding of the spiritual aspects of goods, ownership, possession, gold, and so on, as other parts of the New Testament very strongly indicate. Simon had not yet arrived at a correct understanding of these aspects. He erred, and was duly and severely rebuked. It was not, however, his magic that was being condemned in the Acts, but his misunderstanding of the Christian use of gold and also of the whole business of buying and selling. He had not learned as yet to Christianize his magic – that was the point! But his status as a magician came to be entirely and erroneously mixed up with his sin of simony in the later development of Church thinking, and in a sort of elaborate and historical version of 'Chinese whispers', he eventually ended up as the dark magician Faust who actually did sell his soul to the Devil!

The truth of the matter is that the very early Christians

themselves were also wonder workers, magicians even, but magicians of a new and very different colour than any that had gone before! It would be entirely in keeping with the spirit of the times in which the first followers of the new Way lived to say that they were people who were practising, in every detail of the lives, the white magic of pure spiritual love, a love which poured into their innermost being through their sublime Christ-initiation.

Once, however, the Church lost sight of this initiation aspect of the Mystery, any possibility of ever really understanding the white magic of Christ inevitably got lost to it also. It was, however, essentially this magical and mystery aspect of Christianity which was kept alive in the various esoteric movements, the history of which we have been tracing. And one can say indeed that a sort of Faustian thread runs through all of them.

We will look, therefore, at the Faust story itself now and try to discern something of this elusive thread.

THE STORY OF FAUST

The gist of the story is that Faust, a supposedly real individual who lived in the 16th century, was a highly learned man, accomplished in many of the arts, including and especially, of course, magic. But the implication is that because he could not get fully to grips with the essence of a purely Christian faith and its truth, he decided to sell his soul to the Devil instead. Part of the bargain was that the Devil would duly give Faust the power and possibility to indulge indiscriminately in all his appetites and desires. But his precious soul was the very expensive price-tag!

From the point of view of Esoteric Christianity, it is of no great concern how much or how little of the medieval story of Faust is historically true. There is no doubt, however, that there was a real Dr Faustus who provided the inspiration for what gradually evolved into the legend of Faust. Legends and myths always have some basis in fact anyway, but is it not true that their interest lies as much in the form of consciousness which gave rise to them in the first place as in the details of their expression? In the case of the Faust legend, we have a literary phenomenon indicating the kinds of tensions which had long existed in the soul of Western Christendom but which, however, never achieved any form of true and meaningful expression. Many and varied were the forces which worked both psychically and physically to prevent this from happening ever since the early denial of the essential inner aspect of the Christ Mystery.

It was certainly, however, a very real Dr Faustus who provided the framework of at least an attempted resolution of this great psychological deficiency. Whatever may have been his character in real life, this now proceeded to be embellished imaginatively and ingeniously out of the deepest of Western man's soul-disturbances and spiritual longings. Thus we can see that whatever else he was, Faust was certainly a creature with a very long period of gestation behind him, for when he finally emerges onto the stage of Europe, what we have is a character in which all these conflicting elements in the human soul culminated into a highly moral tale of woe and wonder. The tensions that have now to be dealt with are deep, manifold, and perennial: those for instance between the lower and the higher nature of man; between light and dark; between good and evil, etc. But in the case of the Faust creation, once one understands something of the background and history of esotericism generally, the tensions depicted in him are also very much to do with the spiritual crisis that was becoming increasingly manifest in Europe at this time. For as we have indicated earlier, the Reformation was merely the tip of the iceberg of a far deeper spiritual and religious problem, the origins of which went back to the early Church's eschewing of the real Mystery nature of the Christ. The tensions which this denial engendered within the body of the Church were manifold but were such that they sounded their deepest note in the psychological conflict between man's inner and outer experience, which is also representative of the cleavage between esoteric and exoteric Christianity.

FAUST: SYMBOL OF THE SPLIT PERSONALITY

Herein lies the fascination with Faust and the 'reason' for the emergence of the whole Faust phenomenon at this time. Once the Church's moral, spiritual, and religious authority began to come under the greatest of scrutiny in the 16th century, there also got underway a vital and potentially powerful reappraisal of the ancient wisdom generally. Such a reappraisal lay at the very heart of the Renaissance. Parallel with this development, however, there also arose within Christendom a kind of fear and suspicion of intellectual endeavour generally and of scientific investigation in particular. Up to then the Church had been a sort of protective mother, acting in all aspects of individual human endeavour as a caring guide and a loving teacher. But an understandable fear of the unknown duly arose in the soul of Europe once the individual began to cut himself off from the 'certainty' about the world and the universe that the Church had hitherto provided him with. It was out of this kind of mood that a picture of the Devil then crystallized as a strange yet somehow familiar kind of being, a sort of *doppelganger* who prodded and goaded the human being down all kinds of questionable avenues, tempting him, in the process, towards the most dangerous kinds of accomplishments and freedoms.

The great popularity of Faust, in other words, rested squarely on the fact that he was in a sense a picture of Everyman, insofar as he (Faust) was a representative of a newly emerging type of highly rational consciousness in Europe at this time.

Faust can thus be seen as an imaginative or artistic attempt to get to grips with the huge, even frightening possibilities that this new way of thinking seemed to open up for human beings, especially regarding the material world. Any meddling with God's creation now began to take on a whole new mantle of uncertainty and fear, especially in the souls of those who for far too long had been steeped in a fog of ignorance and superstition.

Small wonder, then, that that band of industrious men who began to emerge at this time, and of whom Faust can be regarded as a prototype, came in for such great misunderstanding and vilification. These were the Alchemists who may correctly be looked upon as the genuine recipients of the ancient wisdom and whose movement (insofar as it may be regarded as such) now became the latest vehicle by which the spirit of Esoteric Christianity would continue to work in the world.

CHAPTER SIXTEEN

THE TRUTH ABOUT THE ALCHEMISTS

The origins of alchemy can be traced way back to the latter part of the first millennium. It was an art, however, which did not, as it were, peak until the 16th and 17th centuries, during which time the greatest of its adepts flourished. Perhaps the best known of these is Paracelsus, who died in 1541.

The Alchemists as a rule were wise, practical, and often very devout men. What distinguished them from other kinds of philosophers or wise men, however, was that they were the first to use the experimental method in the study of Nature. In their own day, they represented the progressive element in many of society's most important and necessary disciplines, including and especially medicine. (Paracelsus's diagnostic method, which was holistic, taking the whole man, body and soul, into account, is undergoing a long-overdue revival in our own day.)

As individuals, they could be adept in many different arts or disciplines. This broadness of their vision and ability was indeed one of the principal features of the Alchemists. They were moreover extremely industrious and laid the foundation for modern chemistry, physics, and science generally.

As materialism advanced in later centuries, however, their reputation fell into disrepute, and they came to be regarded or even discarded as dilettanti, muddled astrologers, quacks, and the like.

There were undoubtedly, as there always are in any profession, dilettanti and frauds among the Alchemists. This element was inevitably blown up, however, by the repressive forces within the Church and society, and was used, in familiar fashion, to discredit, victimize, and, in some cases, even to execute them! Thus, even during their own lifetime they had to exercise extreme caution regarding their practices, for fear of the dreaded Inquisition which was still very active at this time and whose employees were never far out of sight! The great Elizabethan mage, John Dee, for instance, had his fabulous library, museum, and precious instruments destroyed by a mob because they believed he (like Faust!) was conjuring up the Devil!

By the time of the Alchemists' heyday the printing press was in full swing. Consequently, there is a vast spectrum of alchemical literature available, much of it, it has to be said, impenetrable in its symbolism and its allegorical nature. Indeed, it is probable that much of what the Alchemists wrote was purposefully obfuscated so that their knowledge would not become known to the heretic-hunters. What is certain, thanks to modern scholarship and a resurgence of a genuine interest in the Alchemists, is that by and large they were anything but dilettanti. Quite the contrary! They were *the* most serious-minded, cultured, and genuinely spiritual people in an age when much uncertainty existed regarding man's purpose in life and his future on Earth. The Alchemists represented the true spirit-seekers of their age, an age, we must remember, in which Christianity was undergoing the greatest break-up in the West it had so far experienced. Indeed, these two factors, i.e. the break-up of the Church and the emergence of alchemy, are entirely interrelated.

THE ALCHEMISTS AND THE ANCIENT WISDOM

The Alchemists were the true inheritors of the ancient and perennial wisdom. As such they were entirely in tune, both psychologically and philosophically, with the new mood emerging in the human soul at this time. Essentially this was a mood that began to look at Nature in an entirely new way, one of objective, scientific interest.

Alchemy arose out of a blending in the soul of this new mood of pure enquiry into the world with the deepest tenets of the ancient and by now fully Christ-imbued esoteric wisdom. The ancient wisdom, because it is also the perennial wisdom, is always thoroughly alive and never fails to move with the times. (Contrary to popular opinion, esotericism is always ahead of the times rather than behind!) One became an Alchemist, therefore, by taking hold of the esoteric wisdom, as the initiates of old had always experienced and elaborated it, but in an entirely new way. A higher harmony needed now to resound in the soul of those who wished to possess the esoteric wisdom. It was the Alchemists, therefore, more than any of their contemporaries, who attempted to cultivate this sweet harmony in every detail of their lives and work. That this was the case can be easily deduced from the mode of expression they used in their writings, which are often full of the most pious and devout sentiments.

Anyone who approaches the Alchemists with some appreciation of the ancient wisdom will have little difficulty understanding that they were initiates or seers who cultivated assiduously what they called the 'Great Work' and who regarded their very own soul as the true laboratory. For it was there, more than anywhere else, where all the most illuminating experiments took place! The Alchemists were attempting – to express it in another way – to heal the divide between the inner and the outer experience of the world as they perceived it in their individual Christian souls, a division which they felt all the more acutely by dint of the Church's total denial of the esoteric, occult or inner aspect of the Christ Mystery. They were undoubtedly aware (and with varying degrees of understanding) of this anomalous and repressive aspect of the Church's position, and their lives and work were duly tempered by it. It was a problem, however, which they did not succeed in overcoming.

All alchemical activity was regarded by the Church as immoral and sinful, an interference with God's creation. The disappearance and later discrediting of the Alchemists is entirely due to the forces of the Counter-Reformation, which brought about a complete separation of science and religion and paved the way for the eventual triumph of materialism. This one-sided attitude which engulfed Europe in the wake of Newton found it convenient to label the Alchemists, who tried to keep the spirit alive, as dilettantes. It is a label which unfortunately still clings to them in our own day. Nevertheless, the real truth about the Alchemists is slowly emerging as more careful, sensitive, and less materialistic minds turn towards them.

Their main work is generally understood to have been the transmutation of base metal into gold, but it should be remembered that to the Alchemists, gold was as much a Sun-symbol indicating a profound, inner, and essentially spiritual transmutation as an attractive material thing to be sought after for its own sake.

THE ALCHEMISTS SEARCH FOR THE TRUTH ABOUT GOLD

The Alchemists understood evolution through a study of the various metals and mineral substances which they found to be fundamentally related to the different planetary or heavenly bodies. Thus, insofar as the Earth itself is obviously part of the overall cosmic evolutionary scheme, all of the substances which it contains, and especially the metals, could, by an occult law of correspondences, be related to the other planets or heavenly bodies. In this way gold was considered to be a *Sun* metal. And just as the Sun was felt to contain the key to the enigma of the microcosm v the macrocosm, so therefore gold represented the key to the mystery of the universe itself and of man's true relationship to it. We may thus come to understand that the Alchemists had as much interest in the material metal as they had in the Logos-Mystery of the Sun-Being (Christ) whom they held the gold to symbolically represent. In this way, the 'transmutation' which they so earnestly sought may also be regarded as a high degree of initiation into the Sun-Mystery of the Christ. In the *Chymical Wedding of Christian Rosenkreutz* (an alchemical document), there is a scene in which Christian Rosenkreutz receives an initiation through which he is raised to a 'Knight of the Golden Stone'. In alchemy, gold and stone are always profoundly symbolic of the Christ Mystery.

All of this, however, is not to suggest that the Alchemists did not in some cases perform the 'ultimate miracle', and actually transform base metal into gold. The erudite, late 19th century scholar, A. E. Waite, who investigated these matters thoroughly, does not exclude this possibility.[58] However, it was the *deeply spiritual* aspect of their work which, as the Counter Reformation spread and with it the rise of Newtonian science generally, placed the Alchemists entirely under suspicion. For the reactive forces are always, as we have clearly illustrated in the course of this book, set entirely against the spirit and the work of acquiring any kind of true spiritual knowledge and wisdom, a work which invariably draws from them their most resentful and hateful tendencies.

CHAPTER SEVENTEEN

THE ARTISTS KEEP THE SPIRIT ALIVE

As the 17th century progressed and learning and education became ever more widely available, something which was due fundamentally to the increasing supply of printed books, the materialistic bias also became more and more the determining factor of the mass consciousness of Europe. But then, following on the heels of this development, especially from about the 18th century, something else also begins to happen which can be rightly regarded as a fundamental reaction against this materialism. Full-blooded spirituality, as distinct from mere piety, mysticism, or religiosity, now becomes the pursuit of the artist more than any other type of individual.

The Church had always, up to this point, been the primary patron of artists and dictated their themes. But as its moral grip on the mass mind loosened, and the artists evolved more and more freedom of individual expression, they not only saw more and more clearly the truth regarding the Church's sterile relationship with the spirit, but felt an urgent need to express their feelings about it.

So, freed from the restrictive influence of the Church's patronage, the artists in this changing climate began to find new outlets for their work. Book illustration was one of the best of these new 'markets'. The earliest illustration known of the printing press itself (the *Danse Macabre*, printed by Matthias Lyons in 1499) testifies quite well to this emerging trend in respect of the artist and his growing sense of responsibility as the true upholder of the spirit in the modern age.

In this illustration it is Death himself, rather than any other kind of spirit, who is the real inspirer of this new education. The illustration clearly shows how Death is trying to seduce the printers.[59] What the prescient artist depicted in the illustration is quite clear. In effect Death is saying to the book-loving compositors: 'You printers have the pious belief that you are spreading knowledge and wisdom through your books and pamphlets, don't you? Ha, ha, ha. In fact you're doing nothing of the sort! What you're really doing is making me much more alive. Ha, ha, ha.'

The artists begin to feel very deeply at this time that what materialistic science was doing, and indeed could only do, was merely to dissect Nature, and in the process turn her into little more than a machine, or worse, a corpse. Her truly living aspect was being, they felt, completely disregarded. Life itself was being denied. Genuine spirit-seekers, which real artists invariably are, are usually the ones who suffer most from this kind of denial. Indeed, it is the very articulation or expression of this denial which has often been the *raison d'etre* of art, good, bad, or indifferent, since the abandonment of the spirit by the Church.

In short, the artists were alert to an evolving situation in which they could see that materialistic science was discovering genuine secrets of Nature and applying them (for good or ill) to the social sphere. But these secrets, they could also well understand, were of only one side of Nature, her corpse aspect, secrets, that is, of Death itself. This perception, however macabrely the artists may have articulated it, was an inevitable outcome of the abandonment of the alchemical principle of 'inner transmutation'. This principle, which represented the kernel of the Alchemist's work, was based on a study not only of the sub-natural or purely chemical forces contained in the dead matter itself, but more importantly on how those forces could stimulate, into soul-filled life, what was formerly only latent. The Alchemists did not, in this sense, treat Nature as a corpse but rather as a partner in their

'Great Work' of transmutation, a process which was everywhere apparent to their inherently spiritual mode of observation. For when they surveyed the outer world, the Alchemists could see this archetypal process of transformation or metamorphosis at work in Nature's manifold forms. It was a process, however, which, more than anything else, they desired to take effect within the crucible of their own individual souls. The 'Great Work' (Magnum Opus) of the Alchemists always had the ultimate aim of transforming the lower, material, or purely sense-bound man into a higher and truly spiritual one.

But now, within the matrix of 18th century European society, this alchemical mode of comprehension was being denied. This state of affairs was long simmering. It had its theological and philosophical beginnings in the dogmatic declaration at the Council of Constantinople in 869 (see Chapter 10) which denied the existence of the spirit. Now, however, with the newly emerging materialistic science gaining ever greater power in the 17th and 18th centuries, something even more dangerous and sinister was happening. Now the life-giving properties of the very *soul*, as she experiences herself in her intimate communion with Nature, was coming under suspicion, so that not only the spirit, but now also the soul of man was being denied!

ISAAC NEWTON IS CAPTURED BY THE MATERIALISTS

The materialistically-motivated culture which was laying its foundations in 18th century Europe was as dry and soulless an affair as one can possibly imagine, a milieu where only those totally devoid of imagination and given up entirely to pedantry could hope to make any kind of headway in society.

Isaac Newton (1642 – 1727) has long been regarded as the great inspirer of this new, highly utilitarian and mechanistic trend in science and society. But though it is now becoming increasingly obvious that Newton himself was anything but an atheistic pedant, his discoveries in the scientific realm were nevertheless pressed by his followers into the service of this dull, dry culture which became ever more obsessed with one thing, and one thing only – the power and the possibilities inherent in the machine. Thus Mechanism as a general and popular philosophy took hold of the European mind at this time, and the effects of this have remained and have been developing ever since, not just in Europe but all over the world.

It was the artistic movement known as Romanticism which provided the vital antidote to this crass situation. The Romantics felt there was only one way to deal with this soul-destroying mechanism, this paralysis that was gripping Western society, and that was to create one big hell of a stink about it! Stir it all up, was their fundamental philosophy! Make cracks in the system anywhere and everywhere you possibly can, they said, and then maybe, just maybe, some fresh air might get in! Just prior to Romanticism there was an artistic movement in Germany known as the *Sturm und Drang*, which means in effect Storm and Stress! This sums up the mood of the Romantics. Get enthusiastic, get excited about whatever you can. It's the only hope.

Romanticism may not have had much of an effect on

science and religion, but what it did do was instigate a revolution in aesthetic sensibilities, the implications of which are very far-reaching. In a sense this movement has only just begun to colour life in any kind of deep way. Take, for instance, the Romantics' preoccupation with eroticism. Prior to them this was largely unheard of by the mass of Western society. It should be stressed that while it played only a small part in the Romantic Movement also, it is nevertheless perhaps the most obvious legacy of Romanticism in our own culture, although there are many others.

The Romantic Movement is notable in many respects. In terms of the inner life of Western man, however, it is to this movement that credit must go for the survival of any genuine sense of the spirit which we may still possess after the many centuries of suppression. In a world otherwise utterly devoid of spirit, those who longed for its pure and refreshing draught were able to find something of it here in the Romantics, especially in its poets. Insofar as a sense of true Romanticism resides in the modern psyche at all, there resides also a true sense of the spirit.

The Romantic Movement coalesced and developed around a relatively small number of very significant individuals. From the point of view of our present study we will restrict ourselves to mentioning just a few of these. Most notably we must point to Novalis, who, due to a recognition by those who knew him of his profound sense of, and familiarity with, the spirit and the spiritual world, was regarded as the Prophet of the Romantic Movement. He was perhaps all the more highly regarded because he died so young. He was only 29 when he crossed the threshold in

1801. However, the profundity of the small body of work which he left has yet to make its mark. This has largely to do with its deeply spiritual nature, which, when set against the prevailing materialism of our time, is not capable of being properly evaluated. Nevertheless, his nearness to, indeed his deep intimacy with, the Sophia-Christ shines clearly through both his life and his work.

THE TITANIC FIGURE OF GOETHE

Perhaps the full implications of this artistic movement of the Romantics will only be fully recognized in the decades or even centuries to come when another of its luminaries comes into his own, which as yet he has not done by any means, certainly not in the English-speaking, world at any rate. This is the titanic figure of the German, Johann Wolfgang von Goethe, (1749 – 1832), whom we may rightly regard as the greatest genius of modern times.

Goethe is best known today as a poet and particularly as author of the most profound of all treatments of the Faust theme. He worked on his dramatic poem, *Faust*, almost all his life, completing the very complex second part only just before he died. Goethe, however, was much more than a poet. His life and work were perfectly in tune with the spirit of Esoteric Christianity. All his life he was deeply interested in alchemy, and, from the side-lines as it were, vehemently opposed the materialistic trends in the sciences of his day. Apart from being an aesthete, novelist, and poet, Goethe was also an active and productive scientist. His scientific work, however, which drew heavily upon the principles of the ancient wisdom, was not regarded with any real credibility by the establishment of his time, simply because he adopted an approach to Nature fundamentally at odds with the entrenched Newtonian position. His scientific work was actively suppressed. Nevertheless, it is true that Goethe performed most careful and meticulous scientific experiments which unequivocally proved many important things which the materialists did not want to hear. To take perhaps his best example: he proved that Newton's theory of optics is fundamentally flawed.

Apart from anything else that one can say about this, it is a very good example of the sort of materialistic 'mythology' which we still labour under to this day, a kind of hangover, one might say, from the 18th century. For although Goethean science is in our own day beginning to establish itself, Newton's optical laws are still regarded almost universally as being correct and Goethe's as totally wrong! Interesting, maybe, but wrong! What all of this really amounts to, however, is just another case of historical 'Chinese whispers'. None of those who assert, for instance, that Goethe is wrong, ever bother to check him out! If they did they would see that he is in fact correct! What we have here is largely a case of an untruth or a half-truth being taken up and put out by the establishment (for whatever reason), then passed on and on from one person and one book to another, with the inevitable consequences that are always attendant upon untruths or half-truths of this nature. Goethe's *Theory of Colour*, perhaps *the* most accomplished of his contributions in the realm of science, unequivocally proves that colours are not exclusively contained in pure white light as is the Newtonian hypothesis. This is in effect only *half* the picture. In working with the age-old principles of polarity, and the fundamental, reflective relationship of the lower to the higher, of the microcosm to the macrocosm, Goethe proved categorically that colours emerge in their truest nature from the polarity of black and white and not from the pure white light alone.

Thus it can be seen that Goethe's method of scientific investigation differs fundamentally from the orthodox, principally by virtue of the fact that it does not exclude the whole phenomenon for the sake of the expedient particular. The primary trend in materialistic science is always towards isolation. In Goethean science, however, the trend is towards unification. Even more importantly, Goethe does not sacrifice the aesthetic element to the purely utilitarian one. This utilitarian aspect is the primary, almost exclusive feature, of modern science, and from the point of view of our present study may be regarded as decadent. It is decadent because the true ideals of Science are compromised through it to the service of profit-motivated capitalism, and little else. In the personality of Goethe, however, the sublime synthesis of Science and Art is accomplished, and it is for this reason that his life and work are, and will continue to become, an object of the greatest interest to all who wish to pursue a genuine and fully modern spiritual path.

Indeed, Goethean science can be correctly regarded as genuine *spiritual science,* an idea or a concept which materialists have the greatest of difficulty getting their heads around. However, the validity of this assertion regarding Goethe's method can be ascertained from a wide variety of angles, once even a little familiarity with his life and work is gained. But its validity is perhaps best evaluated, in general terms at least, from the fact that in his work Goethe was able to prove scientifically the existence of something which the later psychologist and psychoanalyst Carl Jung (1875 – 1961) was to call the universal spiritual 'archetypes'. These may be regarded as those forces, powers or beings residing in the human soul, a study and an understanding of which throws great light on all the wonderful array of Nature's forms that manifest themselves to us though our physical senses.[60]

GOETHE: MODEL FOR THE FUTURE SCIENTIST

The Goethean method of scientific investigation is thus seen to be holistic. It is rich beyond measure, because it affords a true spiritual insight into Nature. And though it has in recent years just begun to be looked at seriously by the scientific establishment, its long-standing principles are, ironically, very much in accord with the more progressive ideas that are now generally fertilizing the scientific establishment.

One of the principles of the Goethean method of scientific investigation, for instance, is that the investigator must take into account any effect the experiment he makes has on himself (or herself). These effects can never be left out of the overall result of the enquiry. Not only that, but the whole phenomenon of the 'after image' was the subject of the most careful and precise study by Goethe. Once it begins to be understood scientifically, the significance of the 'after image' has powerful potential for thawing the icy grip of materialistic thinking, and allowing the breath of a pure spirit to flow back once again into science, and by extension into life generally. The importance of this holistic approach to all scientific investigation is now slowly becoming recognized, and indeed there is no other way in which conventional science can ever rid itself of its bedevilling 'uncertainty principle' except through it!

All of this, it may very well be argued, seems quite a bit removed from Christianity, esoteric or otherwise. If, however, we are able to appreciate the underlying mood of the Romantic soul, we shall find that Goetheanism is not as far removed from the true spirit of Christianity as we may think at first sight. Considering the situation more closely we will see that there is a spirit at work in all of this which is entirely in accord with the tenets of esotericism. It is also a spirit totally in tune with the basic tenets of the Gospel. For the Gospel is about nothing at all if it is not about total and absolute freedom of the divine spirit as it comes to expression in man. The Romantics for their part most certainly perceived a great threat to this spirit. For theirs was a movement that was, as we have already said, deeply concerned with, was in fact a direct reaction to, the straitjacket into which the whole intellectual life of Europe was forced as the prevailing mechanistic philosophy paved the way for the Industrial Revolution and its horrors.

Romanticism was nothing less than a revolt of the human spirit against all these soul-destroying trends in which they (the Romantics) saw an almost total denial of the mystery element in the Gospel message. And it was now, paradoxically, the case that only they could give a true expression to it.

WILLIAM WORDSWORTH

The great English Romantic poet, William Wordsworth (1770 – 1850) captures something of the Christian mystery element of Nature in his wonderful poem, *Ode to the Intimations of Immortality*, from which the following verse is taken. In the poem, the poet is able to elucidate with great charm, and place into a deeply Christian context, the common but nevertheless archetypal process of physical childbirth and growth, death, and eventual spiritual rebirth. The poem is a profound meditation on the familiar but nevertheless enlightening facts of Nature's great cycle:

Our birth is but a sleep and a forgetting:
The Soul that rises with us, our life's Star,
Hath had elsewhere its setting,
And cometh from afar:
Not in entire forgetfulness,
And not in utter nakedness,
But trailing clouds of glory do we come
From God, who is our home:
Heaven lies about us in our infancy!

Shades of the prison-house begin to close
Upon the growing Boy,
But he
Beholds the light, and whence it flows,
He sees it in his joy;
The Youth, who daily farther from the east
Must travel, still is nature's Priest,
And by the vision splendid
Is on his way attended;

At length the Man perceives it die away,
And fade into the light of common day.

This superb poem, composed of eleven equally evocative
verses, is excellent reading for anyone who wishes to
capture something of the real 'flavour' of Esoteric
Christianity. It is an introduction, as it were, for those who
may not already know much about it, to the foundation of
this ancient spirit of wisdom, wonderfully and creatively
reasserted here for a modern audience through the inspired
work of this poet.

The poem also illustrates very well the deep and genuine
spiritual concerns which lay at the very heart of the
Romantics and their movement. For the whole turning
away from the soul of Nature, a trend which had reached
its nadir in the 18th century, was total anathema to the
Romantics. The eventual outcome of this materialistic
mentality they could well perceive was going to be nothing
less than the very death of the soul and spirit itself.

The Romantic Movement was a direct response to a
gnawing and growing presentiment about the
destructiveness of materialism inherent in its attitude to
Nature. Moreover, the Romantics' presentiment has been
proved entirely correct. For from our retrospective
viewpoint, as we today survey the mass destruction of the
ecosphere, we are witnessing an unsurpassable tragedy
which can be entirely blamed upon the widespread and
prevalent spiritual ignorance we have inherited and which
has culminated in our own greed- and vanity-driven
consumer culture. The true and redemptive love of Nature,
so dear to the Romantics, was and is entirely in keeping
with the Sophia aspect of the Christian mystery, for Sophia

may be regarded as an intrinsic and vital aspect of Nature herself. And it is she who always comes to the fore in any true spiritual revival. This is so because she is, apart from anything else, representative of the true soul of mankind. And in so far as men and women search for their soul and for true meaning in life, they search for Sophia also.

She has been known by many names. For instance, her mystery also figured very strongly in that other great post-medieval movement, the Renaissance, a movement in which esoteric philosophy played a major role. There, however, she was given the Latin name of Natura, perhaps a better or more accessible one, for it indicates how closely connected she is with the wisdom of Nature.[61]

It is also very evident that that towering genius of the Romantics, Goethe, also fully comprehended the vital importance of incorporating this feminine wisdom into Western man's consciousness, if man was to form a true and holistic image of himself and his God. Goethe recognized fully that Sophia lay at the very heart of man's spiritual quest and was the object of the fulfilment of all his deepest and purest desires. The truth of this can be fully gauged from the ending of his monumental work, *Faust*.

In this work, Goethe deals with the whole problem of evil in the most comprehensive and imaginative way possible, and from a deeply Christian viewpoint. Faust goes through his great trials and testings of the Earth, but by the time we reach the final scene:

The noble Spirit now is free
And saved from evil scheming:
Who'er aspires unweariedly
Is not beyond redeeming.

Faust is then borne upwards to the heavenly spheres by the angels and is free at last from all materialistic entanglements, and this is what he experiences:

Free is the view at last,
The spirit lifted:
There women, floating past,
Are upward drifted:
The Glorious One therein,
With star-crown tender,
The pure, the Heavenly Queen,
I know her splendour.

Highest Mistress of the World!
Let me in the azure
Tent of Heaven, in light unfurled,
Hear thy Mystery measure!
Virgin, pure in brightest sheen,
Mother sweet, supernal,
Unto us Elected Queen!
Peers of Gods Eternal!

CHAPTER EIGHTEEN

THE DARK AGE ENDS AND A NEW AGE BEGINS

———ooooOoooo———

The coming of the 19th century saw materialistic science reach its highest, or (depending on how one looks at it), its lowest point. The work of Charles Darwin (1809 – 1882) and the subsequent effect of Darwinian thinking had a profound impact on the life and culture of the West, and especially on its spirituality and religion. Whereas previously man had always, by virtue of his myths and traditions, even by his very nature, looked upwards to God or the Gods for an explanation of his origins, he now turned in the opposite direction and looked for his origins in the natural world only. And so it was that in this mood very clever minds soon began to cast their critical attention upon the Bible and on scripture generally, and particularly on the Gospel itself. It then began to emerge, in the face of a great lack of historically verifiable information, that most of what had been up to this time taken as absolute fact in the Gospels could not be proven 'scientifically'. The materialistic/scientific method of investigation was now, in other words, getting its mechanical claws into the subtle art of history, and the result was little short of a complete debunking of Christianity. A sceptical, satirical, even a downright derisive attitude towards Christianity now became the order of the day in much of the intellectual, artistic, and cultural life of late 19th century Europe. Christianity, and indeed religion generally, was now regarded as merely something for the poor, the ignorant, or the oppressed, a sort of 'opium of the masses', as the most influential of all the materialists of this period (Marx) put it. In this situation it is not surprising, therefore, that intelligent, articulate, and deeply enquiring people in the West now began to seek spiritual nourishment not only outside the Church, but even outside Christianity itself.

The Orient and its treasures of spiritual wisdom had long been known to students of esotericism, but with communications and traffic all the time increasing between East and West, this Eastern wisdom began to make an impact on the West generally. In the process, the Western mind began to wake up to the fact that conventional Christianity was not the be-all and the end-all of religion. Of course, the general mood among the intellectuals regarding Christianity accentuated this East-looking trend. It nevertheless now became obvious that there were vast treasures of spiritual wisdom in Eastern religions quite apart from anything that Christianity could ever offer, treasures moreover which any true and genuine spirituality could not possibly afford to ignore.

MADAME BLAVATSKY, THE GREAT RUSSIAN CLAIRVOYANT

One of the most remarkable public figures of this period was Helena Petrovna Blavatsky (1831 – 1891). A very gifted clairvoyant, Blavatsky wrote very interesting and controversial books packed with arcane and occult knowledge. Her works are a veritable encyclopaedia of esoteric knowledge, but an encyclopaedia which is also, alas, very haphazardly arranged, and because of this, tended and still tends to scare off a lot of methodical intellectuals and scientifically minded people. The publication of these books was nonetheless something of a milestone in the history of esoteric literature, and they were (and still are!) a source of the greatest interest to anyone even vaguely interested in the fascinating subject of the ancient wisdom.

The unprecedented appearance of Blavatsky's books at this time, and indeed her overall motivation, can be explained, in a certain way, out of the ancient wisdom itself. For up to her time esoteric knowledge, when it was published at all, always tended to be allegorical or highly symbolical in form and content. However, the time we are speaking of here, the end of the 19th century, is a point in human evolution when a great 'Cycle of Time' is coming to an end. These Cycles, known as Yugas in the wisdom of the East, where knowledge of them was and is deeply cultivated, run in set periods of 5000 years and are known as (to give apposite examples) Tetra Yuga (Silver Age) and Dvapara Yuga (Iron Age). These immediately preceded the age which was deemed to be ending in the year 1899 and which was known as the Kali Yuga or the Dark Age. So, with the Dark Age ending, and a much more light-filled one dawning, students of esoteric wisdom felt much freer to broadcast their spiritual knowledge and secrets, indeed felt it incumbent upon them now to do so. And this is exactly what Blavatsky did!

She set up in 1875 a Society with the gaol of disseminating as far as possible the principal tenets of the ancient wisdom. This was the Theosophical Society and it is still in existence, though like all the other esoteric societies mentioned so far, quite devoid nowadays of the spiritual quality of its original impulse. In its heyday, however, the Theosophical Society attracted large numbers, and very bright people too, and had branches in many parts of the world. It created a great stir generally, but particularly among genuine spirit-seekers. In a certain sense one can say that if Esoteric Christianity was being cultivated anywhere at this time in any kind of organized way, it was here, under the aegis of this Society. Given the general climate and attitude which existed towards Christianity during its heyday, however, it is not surprising that the Society overtly disavowed any kind of a purely Christian bias. Whereas there was a rich cultivation of the esoteric and ancient wisdom within the Society, there was no real willingness on the part of Theosophists to look at the Incarnation in such a way that its true meaning might be revealed.

Christ was seen by them as merely one of a long line of Avatars or Adepts, no different, basically, from any of the many other great sages and initiates who appear on Earth from time to time. Thus the essential aspect of the Incarnation – its *uniqueness* – was for them never given any genuine consideration. It was this which also spelled the ultimate demise of the Theosophical Society, when one of its leaders, C. W. Leadbeater, became entirely misled by his clairvoyant faculties. This actually happened with Leadbeater regarding Christianity. The resultant downfall of the Theosophical Society occurred in the following way.

Leadbeater was walking in the Indian countryside one day when he came upon a remarkable Hindu boy. The more Leadbeater observed the boy, the more engrossed he became with him. Eventually Leadbeater's faculty of clairvoyance led him to believe that in the boy's aura he was 'seeing' a reincarnation of Jesus! He then proceeded to evolve in his mind a great plan, not only for the boy, but for the Theosophical Society and the whole world! He duly brought the boy before the Society which approved both the plan and the funding of the boy's education in the West. The overall strategy was to eventually announce the boy to the world (when he reached maturity) as the fulfilment of the Second Coming! The boy, however, when he matured and began to understand what was being done to him, found it all extremely difficult. He went through great inner trials and psychic agony. However, he eventually won his inner battles and saw through Leadbeater's megalomaniacal plan. He then denounced it and declared publicly that he was not Jesus but a perfectly ordinary person like everyone else! This happened in 1929. The Society's reputation, needless to say, began to fall utterly apart after this. (The boy, when he grew up, became known as Krishnamurti, and was a highly respected teacher in his own right, up to his death in 1986.)

From the point of view of Esoteric Christianity, this

episode is, in a sad sort of way, very instructive. It indicates very clearly just how very misguided people can become regarding Christ and Christianity, if the essential points of the Incarnation are not properly understood.

The Krishnamurti episode was foisted upon the Theosophical Society by Leadbeater, who had no real understanding of the Incarnation. If he had, he would have known that the physical birth of the Christ was a once only and unique event in the entire history of the Earth planet, something that is set forth with the greatest possible clarity in Rudolf Steiner's Christology.[62] From this it is abundantly clear that what is spoken of in the Gospels as the Second Coming is to do entirely not with the physical body of Christ, but with his mystical or ethereal body. This basic understanding of Christianity is crucial if error regarding the nature of the Real Presence of Christ is to be avoided. The Theosophists, however, in their hot pursuit of Eastern wisdom, eschewed any path that would lead them to such a pure Christian enlightenment.

This is not to say that there were none within the ranks of the Theosophical Society who sensed the fact that Christianity and the ancient wisdom were entirely capable of blending into a new and more enlightened understanding of Christ than was generally available in the West at this time. Whereas there may not have been in the Society any keen discernment of the precise nature of the Incarnation in its purest spiritual essence, there certainly was a sense of something very spiritual in the air. This 'sensing' moreover was not one that was confined merely to Theosophists, either. It had broader repercussions in the artistic and cultural life of the period as well.

THE CELTIC REVIVAL

It was, after all, the ending of the Kali Yuga, the Dark Age! This also coincided very significantly with the blossoming of what we have come to know as the Celtic Revival. There were many enlightened personalities connected with this spiritual/mystical/literary movement, including Fiona MacLeod in Scotland and George Russell (AE) in Ireland, to mention but two.

But of course the chief protagonist of the Celtic Revival was the great Irish poet William Butler Yeats, and from the point of view of our present study it is Yeats who provides us with the most interest.

Yeats is such a broad and complex personality that one hesitates to make any definitive statements about him. Like all of the greatest artists, he is only truly revealed through his artistic work, in this case, his poetry; any attempt to add to that, regarding his personality, risks, one fears, the censure of his very ghost! Although it has up to recently been intellectually fashionable to downgrade the well-known 'mystical dabblings' of Yeats, it pays to remember that it was to these very 'dabblings' that he himself attributed all of the inspiration for his work.

Yeats jointed Blavatsky's Theosophical Society in 1887. However, he found the Madame a bit hard to take, and was later expelled! This, as it turned out, was no great problem for the young William, for he was already a member of another, even more select group of esotericists, and he immediately set about developing his arcane pursuits with them. This was a group of practical magicians known as the Order of the Golden Dawn, and in this Order Yeats found a rich repertoire of myth, symbol, and ritual through which he could enthusiastically set about satisfying his deep thirst for spiritual knowledge and awakening.

And for inspiration, also! Poetry was, after all, the most important thing in life for him then, and this remained the case throughout his life.

True to the intellectual climate of the time, however, Yeats never made much overt use of Christianity in his writing. But this does not suggest that he was not Christian. In fact, it may not be far off the mark to say that his leaving of the Theosophical Society was a 'Christian' impulse. As we shall presently show, it is obvious that he was deeply interested in the mystical side of Christianity and indeed placed it, at one stage, at the very centre of his quest.

The Hermetic Students of the Golden Dawn, to give the group Yeats joined its official title, was founded in 1888 in London, and its repertoire of magical rites and rituals was a sort of potpourri of various mystical and esoteric traditions which had long bubbled under the surface of exoteric Western Christianity. It also took on board some of the extant esoteric knowledge regarding Christian Rosenkreutz, as well as cultivating a sort of latter-day alchemy. In an oath that Yeats took, for instance, as part of one of his 'initiations' in the Order, he had to

> *solemnly promise and swear that with the Divine permission I will from this day forward apply myself unto the 'Great Work' which is so to purify and exalt my spiritual nature that with the Divine Aid I may at length attain to be more than human,*

> *and thus gradually raise and unite myself to my*
> *Magus and Divine genius, and that in this event I*
> *will not abuse the great power entrusted to me.*[63]

As we can see from this, the young Yeats was certainly aiming high! However, that he was deeply aware of the crucial importance of the mystery of the Christ as being central to all genuine esoteric and spiritual pursuits can be deduced from the fact that in 1893 he 'attainted the inner order of the Golden Dawn and in the initiation of the Path of the Portal, he lay down in the tomb, died a symbolic death, and rose reborn in spirit, Christified'.[64]

Fired by his interests and pursuits in Theosophy and the Golden Dawn, Yeats later went on to conceive of a purely Irish esoteric Order which would, he hoped, unite the radical and esoteric truths of Christianity to those of the ancient wisdom. The Order would be called 'The Castle of Heroes'. He developed his plans for this Order to a considerable degree, and had even earmarked an unoccupied castle in the middle of Lough Key in Co. Roscommon as its headquarters. He worked out various rites and rituals for the Order and had some of his friends doing the same. To this Order he hoped to attract the finest specimens of Irish lads and lassies, who would duly receive a thorough esoteric education as well as a deep spiritual training, and in this manner become fit and worthy leaders of their country.

Yeats's plans were highly idealistic and the Order never in fact materialized. But the rites and rituals took on an ever more dramatic or purely artistic form and soon evolved in his imagination into the concept of an Irish Mystical

Theatre. While neither of these projects ever got off the ground, they did bear excellent fruit, for in time they led to the birth of the world-famous Irish National Theatre, the Abbey, which still flourishes.

There is little evidence, however, that as Yeats grew older he deepened his connection with Esoteric Christianity. Rather the contrary seems to have been the case, and he ended his life with a cold relationship to the spirit as perhaps his epitaph shows:

Cast a cold eye on life, on death.
Horseman! Pass by![65]

SOMETHING IS 'IN THE AIR'

The period around the turn of the 19th century was filled with expectation and anticipation. The beginning of any new century is always perhaps a bit like that. However, at this particular turning point there was something 'in the air' which marked it out, certainly from a spiritual point of view, as something quite special. In many ways it was similar to that short period of anticipation and excitement brought about by the Rosicrucian Manifestos when they were initially put into circulation in Bohemia about 400 years previously. But each new 'cycle of time' has its own distinct flavour, its own particular characteristics and impulses, and at the turning of the 19th into the 20th century, with the ever-increasing efficiency of communications, both physically and electronically, a brand-new element made its appearance in the mass consciousness of men: globalization. This feeling, this concept, now began to colour almost every aspect of life, and the result was that a new way of thinking was fast emerging.

Especially in esotericism, this new outlook could be felt in the West as a drawing closer of the East with its rich treasures of spiritual wisdom. Students of esotericism generally were also well aware that the new century represented the ending of the dark age of Kali Yuga, and by virtue of this a new age of light was now being ushered in. George Russell (AE), the Irish visionary, writer, and poet, who was an avid student of the ancient wisdom and a very highly regarded individual in his own day, felt this dawning perhaps more deeply than most. Russell, who was a lifelong friend of Yeats, was one of those rare individuals possessed of a profound though atavistic clairvoyance which allowed him a very special, if idiosyncratic, insight into the true nature of the world and the spiritual beings which underlie it all.[66] It must be said, however, that his temperament caused him to clothe his visions in a deeply Romantic/Celtic way. Unlike Yeats, who kept abreast of the times, AE lost credibility largely because of the stark realism of the progressing century. In his own lifetime, however, he was very much in tune with the overall esoteric/spiritual mood.

Indeed, the whole 'Celtic Revival' of this period, something in which Russell was deeply involved, was very much connected with this awareness of the new post-Kali Yuga age. Insofar as it can be said that the 'Celtic Revival' was concerning itself with a now almost forgotten age some 1500 to 2000 years or more before, it can in many respects be understood as a modern reappearance of the spirit of Esoteric Christianity. If the great friendship between Yeats and AE at this time can be seen in any kind of clear light at all, it must be in the light of the fact that they were both equally deeply imbued with, and inspired by, the pure Sophia or Mother Spirit of their native land. Reviewed in the light of the great mystery wisdom, what else had this ancient land of Hibernia been but a sort of magic cauldron, a Grail, in which the living wonders of the ancient wisdom had fused so wonderfully to produce the prototype, if nothing else, of a great new Christian enlightenment?

Nevertheless, the Celtic Revival was only *one* aspect of a much broader interest in esotericism and spirituality which was 'in the air' at this time. We have already mentioned the very successful Theosophical Society, but this period also saw the setting up, for instance, of the Society for Psychical Research, which attracted a lot of interest. Also at this time there was the big ghostly stirring in more conventional religious circles known as the Spiritualist Movement. There were others.

THE ANTHROPOSOPHICAL SOCIETY

The Theosophical Society was at this time a worldwide society with a very large membership, but was particularly strong in Europe. In Germany, where the deepest of philosophical thinking had always been cultivated and where Christological studies were often very profound, it was only to be expected that the debacle with Krishnamurti would have most serious consequences for the branch of the Theosophical Society there. And so eventually the German branch separated off into a distinct body, under the leadership of the great German-Austrian seer and philosopher, Rudolf Steiner. This new entity later became known as the Anthroposophical Society,[67] and it was in *this* Society, more than anywhere else, that the most progressive awareness of Esoteric Christianity was now being cultivated. The true community and healing aspect of this esoteric spirit can be seen fully at work here in this group, right from its inception, for during the first major global catastrophe, the Great War, Rudolf Steiner, on the neutral soil of Switzerland, gathered hundreds of people from the various warring nations and there instructed them in the building of what may be rightly regarded as a modern mystery Temple.

The building was named, significantly, after Goethe: the Goetheanum. Even a limited acquaintance with this building, the foundation stone of which was laid in September 1913, leads one to conclude that it must have ranked as one of the most fascinating buildings ever constructed. It was a huge building made entirely of wood, and incorporated, among much else within its complex double-domed structure, the whole concept of the microcosmic/macrocosmic relationship of man to the planets and the wider universe.

It was, however, burned to the ground on the night of New Year's Eve, 1922! Given the opposition that Rudolf Steiner met with during his life (there was at least one attempted assassination), it is entirely in keeping with the tragic history of Esoteric Christianity, as outlined in this book, that the Catholic forces of reaction were responsible for it.

As the century progressed, however, these forces became ever stronger. By the middle of the century, after which yet

SEAN BYRNE

another great global catastrophe – the 2nd World War – had
run its course, the entire world became so physically
dejected and mentally numbed that any talk of spirit or
spirituality met with little but disdain. For this war, with
its Holocaust and atomic bombs, combined to effect in the
global consciousness-soul an awful awareness of the evil of
which man was capable, once he had turned his back upon
the spirit of God.

In such an atmosphere, genuine spiritual movements,
especially esoteric ones, had little or no place. By now the
promise of an esoteric spiritual renewal, so widespread at
the turn of the century, had totally dissipated. Virtually all
of man's energy, psychic or otherwise, now became focussed
on mundane needs alone.   An 'Iron Curtain' came down
between the riches that East and West had to offer one
another, and the whole world held its breath as a cold war
of purely materialistic ideologies got under way.

THE SWINGING SIXTIES

The 1960s, however, brought a change to all of this, in the
West at any rate. As the threat of total atomic annihilation
receded somewhat, a new and youthful sense of freedom
duly arose.   A great reservoir of psychic and spiritual
energy, long held in check, was now released in a young,
peace-and-freedom-loving generation. The warmongering
materialistic shell which had cramped the soul's spiritual
longings now burst open once more, this time into a
veritable carnival of new hopes and possibilities.

The Swinging 'Sixties had arrived! What the deeply
searching poets and writers of, say, the Celtic Revival had,

276

in the latter part of the previous century, understood as the ending of the dark Kali Yuga, now took on a whole new extra dimension here of colour, chaos, and spiritual possibility. The New Age was born!

Since then there has been a rich flow of spiritual interchange between East and West, and, especially since the lifting of the Iron Curtain, this augurs well for the future.

A note of caution, however, needs to be sounded amidst the rising tide of a genuine revival of interest in things spiritual. For although the demise of the God-denying ideology of Marxism must, from the point of view of spirituality generally, be seen as an excellent thing, it must also be coupled with an awareness of the rise of fundamentalism in the great world religions, something which most certainly does *not* augur well for the future, as fundamentalism is the perfect breeding ground for terrorists.

With the spiritual release of recent times, however, a rich possibility also is now at hand for the emergence once more, and development to a new stage, of Esoteric Christianity, something which is under way to some extent in any event. Given the aforementioned rise of fundamentalism, if confrontation on a much greater scale between individuals, communities, or nations resulting from religious ideology is to be avoided in the future, it can only be done through a much wider dissemination of the basic tenets of Esoteric Christianity. Fundamental to these tenets is the fact of the promised reappearance or Second Coming of the Christ, which actually begins to happen in our time. This is not, however, a physical phenomenon but an etheric one.

There is no other spiritual philosophy which can unify mankind in the way Esoteric Christianity can. Through it, all are enabled, without prejudice, to tap into and utilize the vital thread of pure spiritual wisdom, the perennial philosophy, which lies at the heart of *all* religions. This, in fact, is what Esoteric Christianity is. Moreover, this is what it *does*. Thus, one can justifiably plead that this form of Christianity be taken up seriously. If this is done, a true and holy Vessel can be forged through which the visionary faculties latent in the human soul can be awakened and nurtured, to the common good of all mankind.

NOTES TO THE TEXT

1   Gnosis is the Greek word for knowledge. Whereas the general term 'The Gnosis' refers more to a period of time, the 'Gnostic Church' is quite specific, and this designation will be used also during the course of this book. The whole of The Gnosis is a fascinating historical period, spiritually speaking, but unfortunately not a lot is known about it, mainly because of all the book-burnings which the Church carried out down the centuries. G. R. S. Mead's fascinating book, *Fragments of a Faith Forgotten*, gives the best available account. The present author's historical novel based on the life of the early Christian philosopher, Origen, and called *Gnosis!* gives an account of the later Gnosis.

2   'Logos' is Greek for 'word.' This Logos aspect of Judaism, and of ancient religions generally, will become clearer as the principal tenets of this book unfold.

3   The 17th century German philosopher, Leibnitz, elaborated in his work the concept of the 'Perennial

Philosophy' (*perennis quaedam philosophia*), which, he believed, constituted a primordial basis for linking science and religion into a unity higher than that which they possess as separate disciplines. In this book, this term and similar ones – most frequently the term 'ancient wisdom' – are used.

4   The word 'spiritualism' in its use here and in other parts of the book is not intended to convey any similarity with its use by the Spiritualist Movement which began in the 19th century.

5   It almost goes without saying that one cannot transmit knowledge about something unless there is a recognized concept regarding the 'something' as a basis for this transmission. Otherwise there is merely muddled thinking! This is largely the situation nowadays with regard to the concept of spirit. This whole book is intended as a contribution towards a renewal of this conceptualizing ability which has been lost through ignorance, as well as through a sustained programme of repression of the spirit or of genuine knowledge of the spiritual world. The other side of the process of achieving certainty regarding knowledge (of anything, including spirit), i.e. actual *perception*, can come about once the thought processes regarding knowledge generally and its acquisition are understood. See *The Philosophy of Freedom* by Rudolf Steiner.

6   Philosophy in the time of Pythagoras still had a Mystery or initiation element to it. Plato (b. 427 B.C.) took this process a big step forward by discussing

philosophy and wisdom much more openly and casually with his students and friends in the gardens of the Academy outside Athens. Hence the birth of 'academic' learning as such, as distinct from Mystery knowledge.

7   'Know thyself, and thou wilt know the Universe and the Gods.' – Inscription on the Temple of Delphi.

8   See Acts 7:22. The first Egyptian name of Moses, according to the Egyptian historian Manethon, was Osarsiph. See *The Great Initiates* by Edouard Schurè, p. 178ff.

9   Ibid, pp. 171-172.

10 Here, for the sake of clarity, in the male/female divide of the Trinity of the Godhead, male is equated with pure divine spirit, and female spirit with what is determined as soul, i.e. the mediating as opposed to the primal spirit, the physical body itself, of course, being the medium.

11 In the Egyptian trinity, the Father, the Solar Word, or Osiris, was also seen as the Sun God. Isis can be regarded as a Moon deity, and their progeny, Horus, pre-eminently became the child of Earth, albeit a Sun-child.

12 *The Great Initiates*, pp. 124-125.

13 A more popular expression of this knowledge was the manner in which the Greek Sun-God Helios was identified with Christ in the early Church. There is a mosaic in the necropolis under St. Peter's in Rome,

dating from the 3rd century, which is known as Christos-Helios. In it Christ is depicted as the God Helios, driving his Sun-chariot across the sky.

14 See Genesis 1:26: 'And God said: "Let us make man in our image." '

15 The traditional symbols for the four Evangelists indicate quite well the presence of this initiation knowledge in the early Church. These symbols have zodiacal and astrological significance and appertain to different types of initiation into the ancient Mysteries. The Bull, for instance, was deified in the worship of Mithras which was very popular in pre- and early Christian times. The symbols are: Matthew (Man), Mark (Lion), Luke (Bull) and John (Eagle). The Gospel in this sense is seen to unify or bring together various aspects of the initiation wisdom through Jesus Christ.

16 See Acts 22:1-21.

17 See Acts 17:23.

18 The Church Father St. John Chrysostom (b. approx. 347 A.D.) addresses 'the initiates' directly in one of his recorded sermons, telling them that they must now learn to deepen their marvel at the Mysteries through the new light and power of Christ.

19 See note 4.

20 As the Church gained ground in the civic world (i.e. in the towns and cities) at the beginning of our era, it gradually came to be regarded as the principal vehicle capable of mollifying the more robust habits of the

countryside dwellers, or even worse, those living on the heaths (hence 'heathens' or 'pagans'). In comparison to the often severe strictness of the literalist Christians, the country people, with their rich and colourful though often licentious habits, thus appeared frightening. Consequently, if they did not join up with the Christians they gradually became disparagingly regarded as mere 'pagans'! In this rejection, however, we have another classic example of the baby being thrown out with the bathwater!

21   This Sun-cult was of Syrian origin and called the Sol Invictus. Through this solar cult, Constantine was able to approach Christianity with far more understanding than would otherwise have been the case, hence his eventual legitimizing of the Christian religion.

22   This is indicated in a number of ways in the New Testament but perhaps the word 'Church' itself, which is derived from the Greek word *Kyrios* meaning Lord, is the best illustration.

23   See Mark 11:15-19; Luke 19:45-48, etc.

24   See Matthew 26:67.

25   See 'Stephen's Defence' in the Book of Acts in the New Testament (specifically 7:48).

26   See *Mystery Knowledge and Mystery Centres* by Rudolf Steiner.

27   See 1 Peter 1:12.

28   See *Mystery Knowledge and Mystery Centres*, by Rudolf Steiner, pp. 128-129.

29   For an imaginative account of Ireland and Britain during the time of Patrick, read the author's work of historical fiction, *Patrick and the Holy Grail*.

30   This is adapted from the version given in *Celtic Myths and Legends* (Rolleston).

31   Attention should also be drawn here to the Wounded King motif, which is a definitive aspect of mythic vision and racial memory worldwide and is especially significant in the Grail legend. It is interesting, however, to note that the wound in the Irish version is much more spiritually explicit than in other versions, where it is in the side or even more pointedly, in the genitalia.

32   See *Celtic Myths and legends* (Rolleston), p. 103.

33   This must be the reason why St. Brigid was the patron saint of milkmaids!

34   *The Great Initiates*, p. 415.

35   This is taken from the wonderful treasure-trove of early Christian spirituality, the *Carmina Gadelica*. This is a huge work of collected songs, hymns, incantations, etc., which was carried out in remote parts of Scotland by Alexander Carmichael and published initially in 1900. All the material was collected from oral recitation by the peasants. Its actual origins therefore cannot be accurately dated, but obviously much of it goes way back to the very earliest period of the Celtic church.

36   *Sun and Cross*, Jakob Streit, p. 201.

37   Ibid., p. 206.

38   Ibid.

39   The sense of self-consciousness which we now take for
      granted is actually a relatively recent intellectual or
      psychological advance. The further one goes back
      beyond the 15th century, the more apparent it is that
      peoples' sense of identity came far more from their
      ancestral or tribal relationships than from their
      individual souls.

40   Erigena means 'Irish born' and the term 'scot' was also
      used to donate Irishness at this time.

41   Polycarp was one of the apostolic Fathers of the Church
      in Asia Minor and was personally acquainted with
      John the Evangelist.

42   See *The Battle for the Spirit* by Canon A. P. Shepherd,
      p. 80.

43   Ibid., p. 73. This is Photius, whose name means 'The
      Enlightened One'. He was 'one of the most famous
      scholars of the Middle Ages and was regarded by post-
      Renaissance philosophers and philologists as the one
      most responsible for making available to Western
      Europe the knowledge of Greek and Hellenistic culture'.

44   Taken from the Canon. See note 42.

45   Avicenna (980-1037) and Averroes (1126-1198), to
      name but two.

46   See *The Ninth Century and the Holy Grail*, W. J. Stein,
      p. 54.

47   See *Letter to the Hebrews*, 7:15-19

48   The name Cathar is a generic term and can be applied
      to a variety of sects, including the Albigenses, active in
      Europe at this time, especially in southern France, but
      also as far away as Italy. We will thus use the term
      'Cathar' from here on to include all of these variations.

49   In the extreme West, however, i.e. in ancient Hibernia,
      things were different. It is well known, for instance,
      that the Druids taught reincarnation.

50   It was also at Troyes in a specially convened Church
      Council in January 1128 that the Knights Templar
      were officially recognized and incorporated into the
      Church as a religious/military Order.

51   The Inquisition was set up by the ascetical order of the
      Dominicans in 1233 to root out the 'foul leprosy' of the
      'pure ones'!

52   The Grail Castle can also be understood in the broader
      context of the Masonic Temple Legend. In this regard
      it is relevant to note that the full name of the Templars
      (rendered into English from the Latin) is The Order of
      the Poor Knights of Christ and the Temple of Solomon.
      Their first preceptory was on the site of the original
      Temple of Solomon in Jerusalem.

53   Philip, during a quarrel over taxes with the Church,
      had imprisoned the Pope in Rome! This was Boniface
      VIII, who died soon afterwards. Philip then installed
      his own Pope (Clement) in Avignon and thus started
      what has been called the Babylonian Captivity of the
      Papacy, which lasted from 1309 to 1377.

54 The two particular societies mentioned here are still in existence, though obviously they are not 'secret' anymore! However, it has to be said that they nowadays bear very little if indeed any resemblance in character, function, or spiritual content to the old or original societies from which they take their names. See, in this regard, especially *The Rosicrucian Enlightenment* by Francis Yeats, which gives an extremely broad historical overview of the profound influence and significance of the original Rosicrucian Brotherhood.

55 The word 'utopia' is from the Greek and means 'no place'.

56 See note 57.

57 The word 'imaginative' or 'imagination' in this special context is not intended to convey the usual meaning of something unreal or of the nature of fantasy, but rather that form of consciousness only by which truly spiritual realities may be apprehended.

58 The Alchemists Through the Ages by A. E. Waite, p. 33.

59 In the beginning of printing, the printer mattered far more than the author of the book.

60 Students of Goethean science are familiar with what Goethe called the *urpflanze*, the archetypal plant. This, however, unlike Jung's archetypes, Goethe did not regard merely as an hypothesis, but something he could see in reality, due to the training he undertook for his experimental method.

61   The name Pansophia was also coined in the 17th century by one of this period's most enlightened minds, Comenius. This is an excellent name also for it joins the male god of Nature, Pan, with the essentially feminine or soul-wisdom of the natural world, giving us the more inclusive and 'Europeanised' Pansophia.

62   Steiner lectured extensively on Christianity and many of his lectures are collected and available in book form, unrevised, however, by him. Moreover, most of these require a thorough knowledge of his fundamental philosophy in order to be fully understood. However, his written work, *Christianity As Mystical Fact*, gives an outline of his Christology for the general reader.

63   *Yeats – The Man and the Masks,* R. Ellman, p. 99.

64   Ibid.

65   This is inscribed on Yeats's tombstone in the church graveyard at Drumcliff, Co. Sligo.

66   For a wonderful and moving account of how Russell's clairvoyant faculty opened, and how subsequently through this awakening he gained such a splendid vision and insight into the spiritual world and its angelic inhabitants, read his book, *The Candle of Vision*, which has become a modern spiritual classic.

67   This Society is still flourishing and directs a growing worldwide movement through which genuine spiritual impulses are being brought to bear on the arts, sciences, and religions of various cultures and peoples. It is a movement dedicated to the ideal of the spiritual

regeneration of modern civilization. See *Rudolf Steiner: Herald of a New Epoch* by Stewart Easton.

SELECT BIBLIOGRAPHY

Adamson, Ian, *Bangor, Light of the World*, Pretani Press, 1987.

Adomnan's *Life of Columba*, A. O. and M. O. Anderson (Eds.), Thomas Nelson and Sons Ltd., 1961.

A. E. (George Russell), *Candle of Vision*, Aziloth Books, 2012.

Archiati, Pietro, *The Great Religions*, Temple Lodge, 1998.

Baigent, Michael and Leigh, Richard, *The Elixir and the Stone*, Viking, 1997.

Bamford, Christopher and Marsh, William Parker (Eds.), *Celtic Christianity: An Anthology*, Floris Classics, 1986.

Bennell, Margaret and Wyatt, Isabel, *The Chymical Wedding of Christian Rosenkreutz (A Commentary)*, Temple Lodge, 1989.

Betti, Mario, *The Sophia Mystery in our Time*, Temple Lodge, 1994.

Blavatsky, H. P., *Isis Unveiled*, Theosophical University Press (USA), 1960.

Byrne, Sean, *Gnosis!* Age-Old Books, 2017.

Byrne, Sean, *Patrick and the Holy Grail*, Age-Old Books, 2016.

Carmichael, Alexander, *Carmina Gadelica*, Floris Books, 1992.

Christie-Murray, David, *A History of Heresy*, London, 1976.

Curtayne, Alice, *St. Brigid of Ireland*, Sheed & Ward (USA), 1954.

DiCarlo, Russel, E. (Ed.), *Towards a New World-View*, Floris Books, 1996.

Easton, Stewart, *Rudolf Steiner: Herald of a New Epoch,* The Anthroposophic Press (USA), 1980.

Ellmann, Richard, *Yeats: The Man and the Masks*, Penguin Books, 1979.

Erigena, John Scotus, *The Voice of the Eagle* (Trans: Christopher Bamford), Lindisfarne Press, 1990.

Eschenbach, Wolfram von, *Parzival*, Vintage Books (USA), 1961.

Frieling, Rudolf, *Christianity and Reincarnation*, Floris Books, 1977.

Goethe, Johann Wolfgang von, *Faust*, Parts 1 & 2, (Trans: Bayard Taylor), Sphere Books, 1969.

Guthrie, Kenneth Sylvan, *The Pythagorean Sourcebook and Library*, Phanes Press (USA), 1987.

Head, Joseph, & Sranston, S. L. (Eds.), *Reincarnation: An*

East-West Anthology, The Julian Press (USA), 1961.

Holms, Edmond, *The Holy Heretics*, Watts, 1948.

Lowndes, Floris, *Enlivening the Chakra of the Heart,* Sophia Books, 1998.

Marsden, John, *Sea-Road of the Saints*, Floris Books, 1995.

Matthews, John, *The Grail – Quest for the Eternal*, Thames and Hudson, 1981.

Mead, G. R. S., *Fragments of a Faith Forgotten*, University Books, (USA), 1960.

Naydler, Jeremy, *Goethe on Science – An Anthology*, Floris Books, 1996.

Novalis, *Hymns to the Night & Spiritual Songs*, Temple Lodge Press, 1992.

O'Donohue, John, *Anam Cara*, Bantam Books, 1999.

Oldenburg, Zoe, *Destiny of Fire*, Penguin Books, 1969.

Pagels, Elaine, *The Gnostic Gospels*, Random House, 2006.

Proskauer, Heinrich O., *The Rediscovery of Colour – Goethe versus Newton Today*, Anthroposophical Press (USA), 1986.

Pseudo-Dionysius, *The Complete Works* (Trans: Colm Luibheid), Paulist Press (USA), 1987.

Rolleston, T. W., *Celtic Myths and Legends*, Studio Editions Ltd., 1994.

Ryan, John, *Irish Monasticism*, Four Courts Press, 1992.

Saint Patrick, Iain McDonald (Ed.), Floris Books, 1992. (This book contains the *Confession*).

Schurè, Edouard, *From Sphinx to Christ*, Rudolf Steiner Publications (USA), 1970.

Schurè, Edouard, *The Great Initiates*, Steinerbooks (USA), 1976.

Seddon, Richard, *The Mystery of Arthur at Tintagel*, Rudolf Steiner Press, 1990.

Shepherd, Canon A. P., *Battle for the Spirit*, Anastasi Ltd., 1994.

Stein, W. J., *The 9th Century and the Holy Grail*, Temple Lodge Press, 1988.

Steiner, Rudolf, *The Reappearance of Christ in the Etheric,* The Anthroposophic Press (USA), 1970.

Steiner, Rudolf, *Mystery Knowledge and Mystery Centres*, Rudolf Steiner Press, 1973.

Steiner, Rudolf, *The Philosophy of Freedom*, Rudolf Steiner Press, 1988.

Streit, Jakob, *Sun and Cross*, Floris Books, 1993.

Tagore, Rabindranath, *Gitanjali (Song Offerings)*, Macmillan and Co., 1914.

Underhill, Evelyn, *Mysticism – The Nature and Development of Spiritual Consciousness*, Oneworld Publications Ltd., 1993.

Van Der Post, Laurens, *Jung, and the Story of Our Time*, The Hogart Press, 1976.

Versluis, Arthur, *Theosophia*, Lindisfarne Press (USA), 1994.

Waite, A. E., *The Alchemists Through the Ages*, Rudolf Steiner Publications (USA), 1970.

Welburn, Andrew J., *The Truth of Imagination*, Macmillan, 1989.

Williams, Charles, *War in Heaven*, William B. Eerdman (USA), 1949.

Wordsworth's Verse (selected by R. S. Thomas), Faber and Faber, 1971.

Yates, Frances A., *The Rosicrucian Enlightenment*, Routledge and Keegan Paul, 1972.

Yeats, W. B., *Collected Poems*, Macmillan and Co., 1952.

#0003 - 290817 - C0 - 203/127/16 - PB - 9780954025557